SOCCER LEGENDS

MEN'S 2027

PUBLISHED IN THE USA IN 2026 BY WELBECK CHILDREN'S BOOKS
An imprint of Hachette Children's Group
Part of Hodder & Stoughton Limited
Carmelite House, 50 Victoria Embankment, London, EC4Y 0DZ
An Hachette UK Company
www.hachette.co.uk
www.hachettechildrens.co.uk

FSC
www.fsc.org
MIX
Paper | Supporting responsible forestry
FSC® C104740

All statistical data and player heat maps provided by Opta, under license from Stats Perform.

10 9 8 7 6 5 4 3 2 1
ISBN 978 1 83955 334 9

Printed and bound in China
Author: David Ballheimer
Senior Commissioning Editor: Suhel Ahmed
Design Manager: Matt Drew
Picture research: Paul Langan
Production: Melanie Robertson

PICTURE CREDITS
The publishers would like to thank the following sources for their kind permission to reproduce the pictures in this book.

ALAMY: ANP 17; Beautiful Sports Pressphoto Agency 70; Bagu Blanco/Pressinphoto 89; Mickael Chavet/Zuma Press 105; Craig Cowan/Every Second Media 110B; dpa picture alliance 94; Mike Egerton/PA 10, 91; Rich Graessle/Icon Sportswire 80; Marco Iacobucci 98; Lee Keuneke/Every Second Media 111T; Alex Lopez 19; Giuseppe Maffia 45; Andrew Milligan/PA 48; Jonathan Moscrop/Sportimage 65; Cesar Ortiz/Pressinphoto 43; Bruna Prado/AP 77; UPI 33; John Walton/PA 14

GETTY IMAGES: AC Milan 52; Robin Alam/ISI Photos 47; Ion Alcoba/Quality Sport Images 56; Eric Alonso/UEFA 9; Emilio Andreoli 20; ANP 36, 55, 72; Franco Arland/UEFA 35; Matias Baglietto/NurPhoto 46; Lars Baron 57; Robbie Jay Barratt/AMA 67, 97; James Baylis/AMA 109T; Berengui/DeFodi Images 8; John Berry 21, 88; Mark Blinch 60; Stefan Brauer/DeFodi Images 106T; Megan Briggs 74; Rico Brouwer/Soccrates 13; Clive Brunskill 12; David S. Bustamante/Soccrates 22, 78; Pedro Castillo/Real Madrid 34; Jean Catuffe 16, 82, 100; Tim Clayton/Corbis 39; Gareth Copley 106B; Oscar Del Pozo/AFP 111B; Sebastian El-Saqqa - firo sportphoto 18; Paul Ellis/AFP 85, 109B, 110T; Gualter Fatia 62; Johnny Fidelin/Icon Sport 83; Franck Fife/AFP 27; Stuart Franklin 90, 99; Sebastian Frej/MB Media 64; Edith Geuppert/GES Sportfoto 38; James Gill/Danehouse 81; GSI/Icon Sport 50; Stefano Guidi 102; Lionel Hahn 108T; Alexander Hassenstein 95; Mike Hewitt 59; Image Photo Agency 42; Catherine Ivill 11; Fareed Kotb/Anadolu 49; Roland Krivec/DeFodi Images 31; Harry Langer/DeFodi Images 24; Alex Livesey 63, 103; Stuart MacFarlane/Arsenal FC 54, 107T; Angel Martinez 26, 61; Wagner Meier 29; Doug Murray/Icon Sportswire 28; Rene Nijhuis/MB Media 75; Mattia Ozbot/Inter 23; Alex Pantling 40; Ryan Pierse 101; Andrew Powell/Liverpool FC 7; Antonio Pozo/Pressinphoto/Icon Sport 68; Pressinphoto/Icon Sport 44; Joe Prior/Visionhaus 15, 51; Quality Sport Images 87, 96; Michael Regan 86, 107B; Maciej Rogowski/Eurasia Sport Images 92; Oli Scarff/AFP 5; Silas Schueller/DeFodi Images 69; Juan Manuel Serrano Arce 108B; Justin Setterfield 93; Alexandre Simoes/Borussia Dortmund 37; Nick Tre. Smith/Icon Sportswire 25; Boris Streubel 73; Justin Tallis/AFP 53; Pedro Vilela 76; Visionhaus 41, 66, 71, 79; Damjan Zibert/Soccrates 30

Every effort has been made to acknowledge correctly and contact the source and/or copyright holder of each picture; any unintentional errors or omissions will be corrected in future editions of this book.

All facts and stats correct as of July 2026

SOCCER LEGENDS

MEN'S 2027

STATS • PROFILES • TOP PLAYERS

WELBECK
CHILDREN'S BOOKS

CONTENTS

HOW THE STATS WORK

Welcome to Men's Soccer Legends 2027, the book packed with stats, facts, and heat maps for more than 100 of the biggest names in soccer today.

Inside, you'll find star defenders, midfielders, forwards, goalkeepers, and managers from the world's top five European leagues: the Bundesliga in Germany, La Liga in Spain, Ligue 1 in France, Serie A in Italy, and the Premier League in England. Some are playing in those leagues now, while others have spent most of their careers there up to the 2025–26 season.

Want to compare the greats? Start with the stats. Every position has a different job, so each section focuses on different skills. Defenders are measured on how they stop attacks. Forwards are judged on goals, assists, and attacking danger. Goalkeepers are tested on saves, crosses, passing, and how they protect their area.

Check out the heat maps too. They show where each player spends most of his time on the field. For goalkeepers, the heat maps reveal who stays close to the goal and who races farther out as a sweeper-keeper.

The stats cover each player's career so far, focusing on domestic league and European games for clubs in the top five European leagues. They don't include domestic cups, super cups, and international games. This keeps the data fair and easy to compare, so you can decide who really deserves to be called a legend of the game.

DEFENDERS

A defender's job is to prevent the opposing team from scoring by protecting his own goal. There are many different types of defenders (and defensive formations too) and their positions demand different skills. Full-backs play out wide and are quick and agile; they try to stop wingers and wide midfielders from delivering crosses into the penalty area. Center-backs are in the middle; they are often strong and tall so they can win the ball from dangerous forwards. Wing-backs are like full-backs, but they play in a more forward role and also attack like wingers. Teams sometimes use a spare defender called a "sweeper" who plays behind the center-backs and offers extra protection.

WHAT DO THESE STATS MEAN?

AERIAL DUELS WON

This is the percentage of headers a defender has won in his own penalty area, to interrupt an opposition attack.

INTERCEPTIONS

This is the number of times a defender has successfully stopped an attack without needing to make a tackle.

BLOCKS

A shot that is intercepted by a defender—preventing his keeper from having to make a save—counts as a block.

KEY PASSES/PASS COMPLETION

A key pass is one that results in an attacking opportunity. Pass completion indicates as a percentage the player's passing accuracy.

CLEARANCES

An attack successfully foiled, either by kicking or heading the ball away from danger, counts as a clearance.

TACKLES

This is the number of times a defender has challenged and dispossessed the opposition without committing a foul.

Did you know?

The last defender to win the Ballon d'Or, or the FIFA World's Best Player award, was Italy's Fabio Cannavaro in 2006. Only Virgil van Dijk in 2019 was voted in the top three players since 2010.

DAVID ALABA

NATIONALITY
Austria

CURRENT CLUB
Real Madrid

4

David Alaba's biggest strengths are his reading of the game and his versatility. He is most at home at left-back, but can play in several defensive roles. Quick, athletic, and calm on the ball, he spots danger early and can turn defense into attack in seconds.

DATE OF BIRTH	JUN 24, 1992
POSITION	LEFT-BACK
HEIGHT	5 FT, 11 IN
PRO DEBUT	2007
PREFERRED FOOT	LEFT

APPEARANCES	511
INTERCEPTIONS	607
GOALS	34
TACKLES	597
CLEARANCES	713
PASSES	29,809
PENALTIES SCORED	3
BLOCKS	156
AERIAL DUELS WON	49.6%
PASS COMPLETION	89.2%

MAJOR CLUB HONORS

⚽ La Liga: 2022, runner-up 2023, 2024 ⚽ Bundesliga: 2010, 2013–2021 (all B. Munich.) ⚽ UEFA Champ. League.: 2013, 2020 (all B. Munich), 2022, 2024 ⚽ FIFA Club World Cup: 2013, 2020 (all B. Munich), 2022 ⚽ Copa del Rey: 2023 ⚽ DFB-Pokal: 2013, 2014, 2016, 2019, 2020 (all B. Munich)

INTERNATIONAL HONORS

⚽ None to date

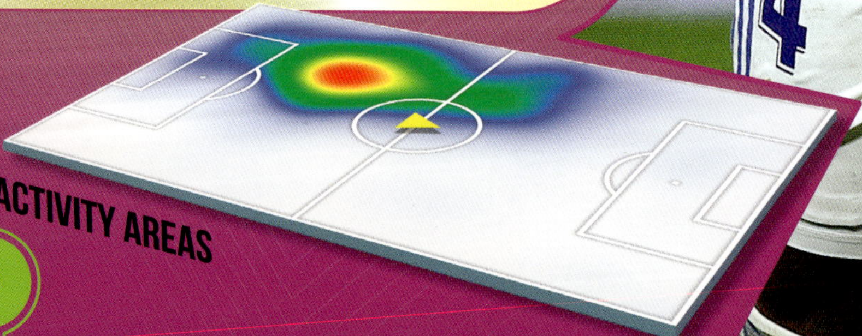

ACTIVITY AREAS

TRENT ALEXANDER-ARNOLD

NATIONALITY
England

CURRENT CLUB
Real Madrid

Trent Alexander-Arnold is a brilliant right-sided player with excellent technique and passing range. He can play at right-back, wing-back, or farther forward in midfield. His runs down the flank are dangerous, and his pinpoint crosses can create chances from almost anywhere.

DATE OF BIRTH	OCT 7, 1998
POSITION	FULL-BACK
HEIGHT	5 FT, 9 IN
PRO DEBUT	2016
PREFERRED FOOT	RIGHT

APPEARANCES 360
INTERCEPTIONS 420
GOALS 20
TACKLES 588
CLEARANCES 490
PASSES 20,496
PENALTIES SCORED 0
BLOCKS 57

AERIAL DUELS WON 38.2%
PASS COMPLETION 78.3%

MAJOR CLUB HONORS
⚽ Premier League: 2020, 2025 (all Liverpool) ⚽ UEFA Champions League: 2019 (Liverpool) ⚽ UEFA Champions League: runner-up 2018, runner-up 2022 (all Liverpool) ⚽ FIFA Club World Cup: 2019 (Liverpool) ⚽ FA Cup 2022 (Liverpool)

INTERNATIONAL HONORS
⚽ UEFA Nations League: third place 2019
⚽ UEFA European Championship: runner-up 2024

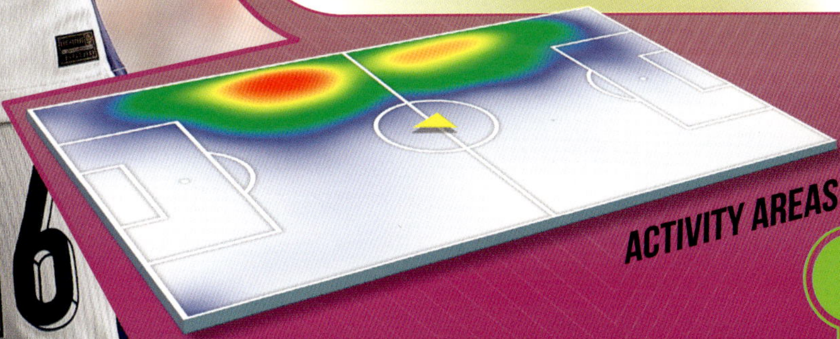

ACTIVITY AREAS

NATIONALITY
Italy

CURRENT CLUB
Inter Milan

ALESSANDRO BASTONI

A classy left-footed center-back, Bastoni is a key part of Inter's defense and Italy's back line. Strong in the air and calm on the ball, he can stop attacks, carry possession forward, and pick smart passes. In 2025–26, he helped Inter win Serie A again.

DATE OF BIRTH	APR 13, 1999
POSITION	CENTER-BACK
HEIGHT	6 FT, 3 IN
PRO DEBUT	2006
PREFERRED FOOT	LEFT

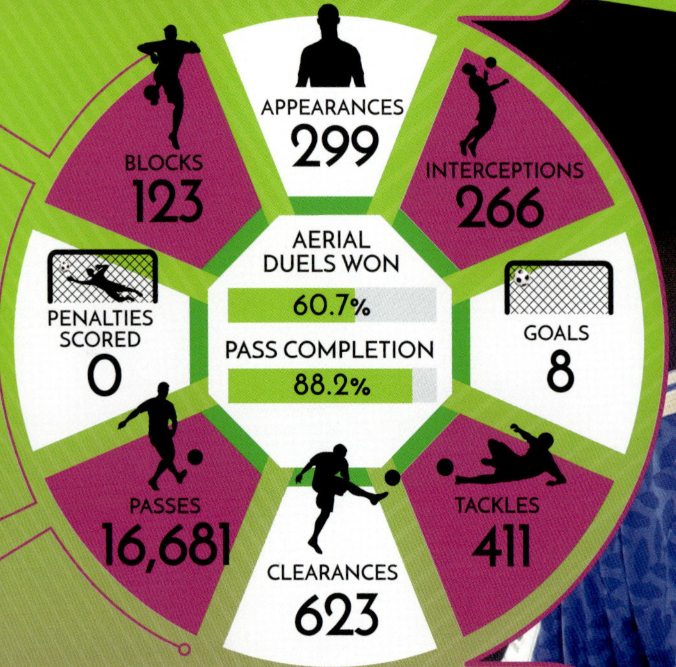

MAJOR CLUB HONORS

⚽ Serie A: 2021, 2024, 2026 ⚽ UEFA Champions League: runner-up 2023, 2025 ⚽ UEFA Europa League: runner-up 2020 ⚽ Coppa Italia: 2022, 2023, 2026 ⚽ Supercoppa Italiana: 2021, 2022, 2023

INTERNATIONAL HONORS

⚽ UEFA European Championship: 2020
⚽ UEFA Nations League: third place 2021

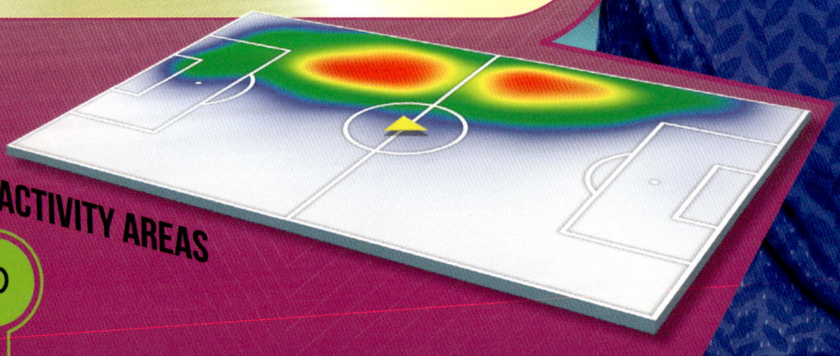

ACTIVITY AREAS

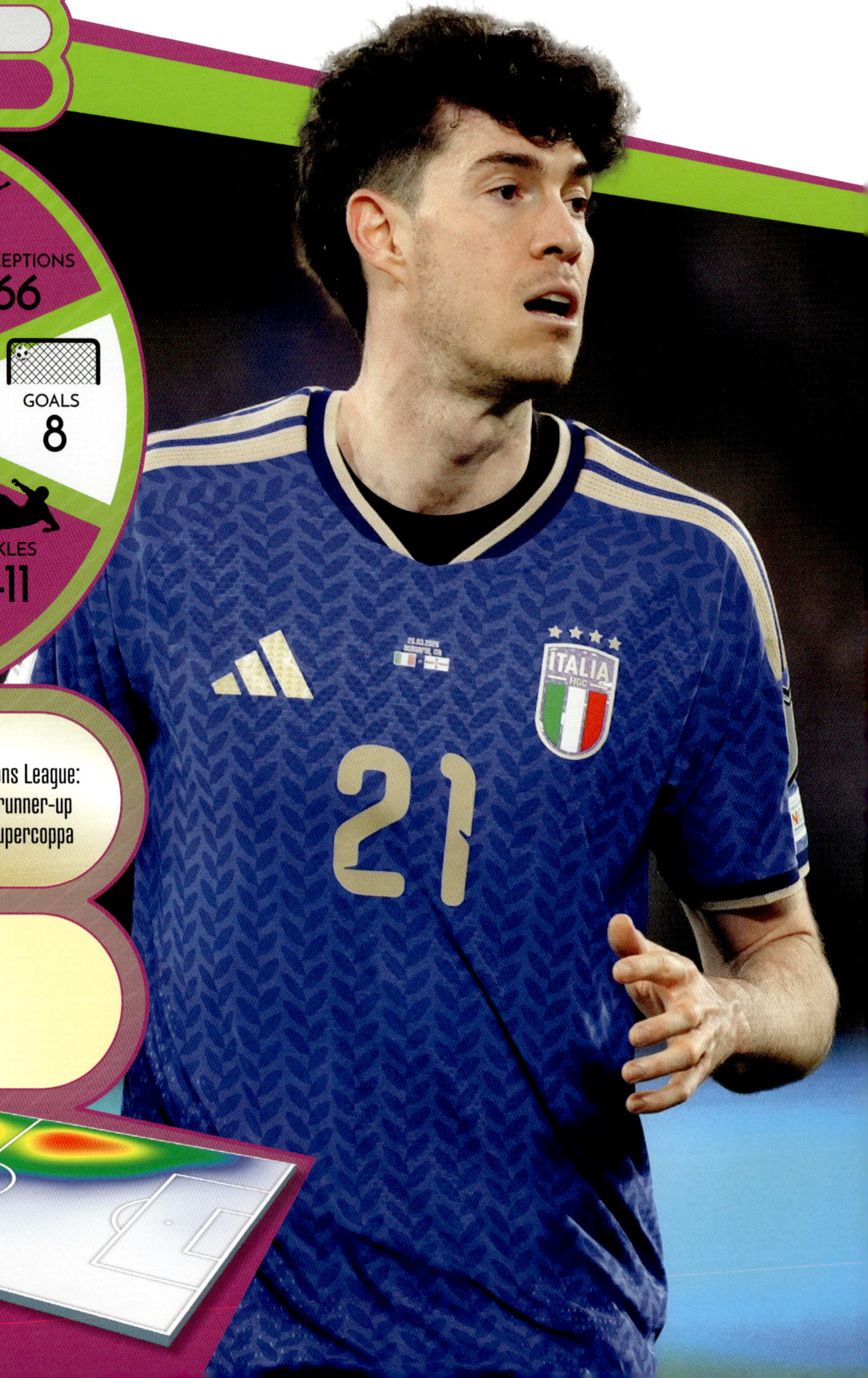

RÚBEN DIAS

A commanding center-back, Dias was a key part of Manchester City's Treble-winning team in 2023. Calm on the ball and powerful in the air, he can start attacks from deep, pick out passes, and clear danger when crosses fly into the box.

NATIONALITY
Portugal

CURRENT CLUB
Manchester City

DATE OF BIRTH	MAY 14, 1997
POSITION	CENTRAL
HEIGHT	6 FT, 2 IN
PRO DEBUT	2015
PREFERRED FOOT	RIGHT

APPEARANCES 339
BLOCKS 195
INTERCEPTIONS 310
AERIAL DUELS WON 58.1%
PASS COMPLETION 91.7%
PENALTIES SCORED 0
GOALS 17
PASSES 24,776
CLEARANCES 962
TACKLES 370

MAJOR CLUB HONORS
- Premier League: 2021, 2022, 2023, 2024
- UEFA Champions League: runner-up 2021, 2023
- Portuguese Premier Liga: 2019 (Benfica)
- FA Cup: 2023, runner-up 2025, 2026

INTERNATIONAL HONORS
- UEFA Nations League: 2019

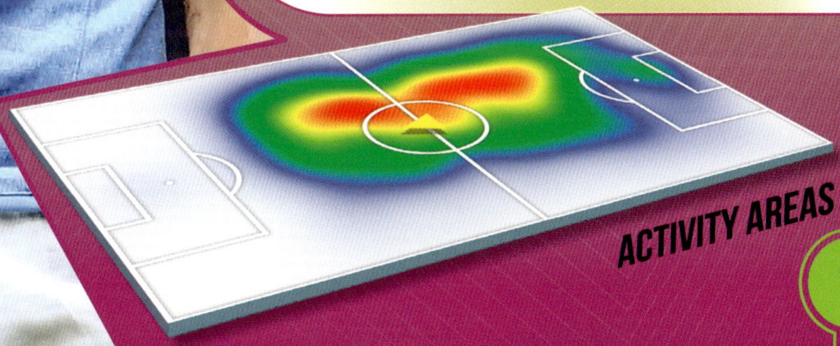
ACTIVITY AREAS

VIRGIL VAN DIJK

4

NATIONALITY
Netherlands

CURRENT CLUB
Liverpool

Regarded as one of the best central defenders of his generation, Virgil van Dijk's is a calm presence on the field which makes him a great leader. He has great positional sense and frequently breaks up attacks. He can also get on to the end of set pieces, making him dangerous in the opposition box.

DATE OF BIRTH	JUL 8, 1991
POSITION	CENTRAL
HEIGHT	6 FT, 5 IN
PRO DEBUT	2011
PREFERRED FOOT	RIGHT

APPEARANCES 491*
INTERCEPTIONS 690
GOALS 45
TACKLES 517
CLEARANCES 2,706
PASSES 32,892
PENALTIES SCORED 0
BLOCKS 277
AERIAL DUELS WON 74.4%
PASS COMPLETION 88.3%

*Excludes data from Scottish Premiership

MAJOR CLUB HONORS

⚽ Premier League: 2020, 2025 ⚽ Scottish Premiership: 2014, 2015 (Celtic) ⚽ UEFA Champions League: 2019, runner-up 2018, runner-up 2022 ⚽ FIFA Club World Cup: 2019 ⚽ FA Cup: 2022

INTERNATIONAL HONORS

⚽ UEFA Nations League: runner-up 2019

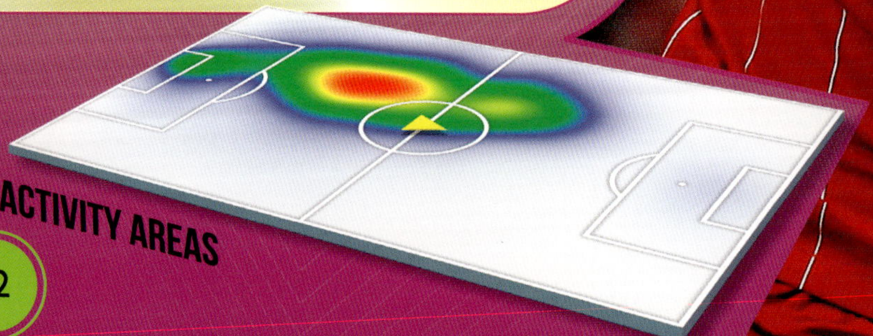

ACTIVITY AREAS

JEREMIE FRIMPONG

A flying wing-back with explosive pace, Frimpong can also push into midfield and help build attacks. After starring on Bayer Leverkusen's unbeaten Bundesliga-winning team, he brought his speed, sharp passing, and smart movement to Liverpool.

NATIONALITY
Netherlands

CURRENT CLUB
Liverpool

30

DATE OF BIRTH	DEC 10, 2000
POSITION	RIGHT WING-BACK
HEIGHT	5 FT, 8 IN
PRO DEBUT	2019
PREFERRED FOOT	RIGHT

APPEARANCES 211*
INTERCEPTIONS 83
GOALS 27
TACKLES 219
CLEARANCES 164
PASSES 5,559
PENALTIES SCORED 0
BLOCKS 15
AERIAL DUELS WON 37.4%
PASS COMPLETION 82.3%

*Excludes data from Scottish Premiership

MAJOR CLUB HONORS

⚽ Bundesliga: 2024 (Bayer Leverkusen) ⚽ UEFA Europa League: runner-up 2024 (Bayer Leverkusen) ⚽ DFB-Pokal 2024 (Bayer Leverkusen) ⚽ Scottish Premiership: 2020 (Celtic) ⚽ Scottish Cup: 2020 (Celtic)

INTERNATIONAL HONORS

⚽ UEFA Nations League: runner-up 2019

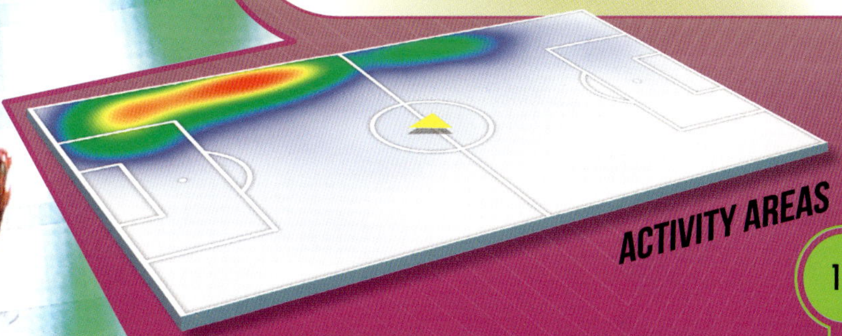

ACTIVITY AREAS

6

NATIONALITY
Brazil

CURRENT CLUB
Arsenal

GABRIEL

A strong and fearless center-back, Gabriel is a huge part of Arsenal's rock-solid defense. Powerful in the air, tough in tackles, and calm on the ball, he can shut down dangerous forwards and pass neatly from the back. In 2025, he signed a new long-term Arsenal contract.

DATE OF BIRTH	DEC 10, 1997
POSITION	CENTER-BACK
HEIGHT	6 FT, 3 IN
PRO DEBUT	2016
PREFERRED FOOT	LEFT

APPEARANCES	282
INTERCEPTIONS	223
GOALS	25
TACKLES	346
CLEARANCES	1,005
PASSES	16,611
PENALTIES SCORED	0
BLOCKS	234
AERIAL DUELS WON	60.6%
PASS COMPLETION	87.9%

MAJOR CLUB HONORS

- FA Premier League: 2026
- UEFA Champions League: TBC
- Prva HNL 2018 Dinamo Zagreb

INTERNATIONAL HONORS

- None to date

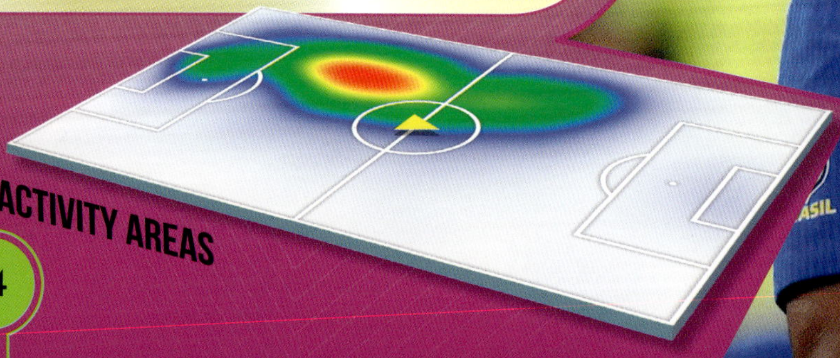

ACTIVITY AREAS

NEW ENTRY!

JOŠKO GVARDIOL

Quick, strong, and smart, Gvardiol is a nightmare for attackers in one-on-one battles. He times his tackles well, blocks bravely, and reads passes before danger can grow. Once he wins the ball, he has the skill to drive forward and start attacks.

NATIONALITY
Croatia

CURRENT CLUB
Manchester City

DATE OF BIRTH	JAN 23, 2002
POSITION	CENTRAL
HEIGHT	6 FT, 1 IN
PRO DEBUT	2019
PREFERRED FOOT	LEFT

APPEARANCES 194
INTERCEPTIONS 242
GOALS 18
TACKLES 275
CLEARANCES 442
PASSES 12,919
PENALTIES SCORED 0
BLOCKS 93
AERIAL DUELS WON 56.4%
PASS COMPLETION 88.6%

MAJOR CLUB HONORS
⚽ Premier League: 2024 ⚽ DFB Pokal: 2022, 2023 (RP Leipzig) ⚽ UEFA Super Cup: 2023 ⚽ FIFA Club World Cup: 2023

INTERNATIONAL HONORS
⚽ FIFA World Cup: third place 2022
⚽ Copa América third place 2024

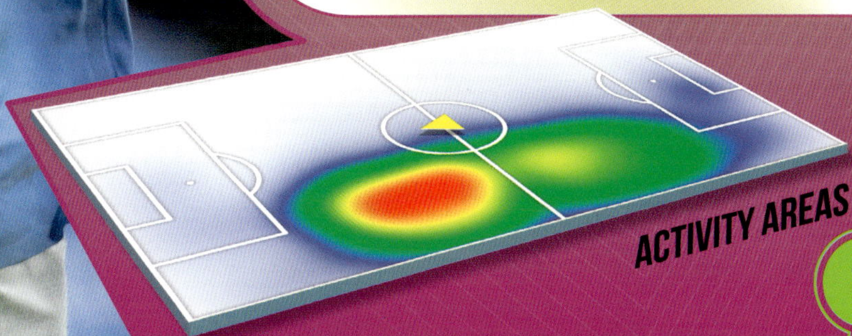

ACTIVITY AREAS

ACHRAF HAKIMI

2

NATIONALITY
Morocco

CURRENT CLUB
Paris Saint-Germain

One of the world's best right-backs, Hakimi is a flying defender who can also push into midfield. His incredible pace helps him race back to stop attacks, then burst forward to trouble opponents. In 2025, he helped Morocco win the Africa Cup of Nations and was named African Footballer of the Year.

DATE OF BIRTH	NOV 4, 1998
POSITION	RIGHT-BACK
HEIGHT	5 FT, 11 IN
PRO DEBUT	2016
PREFERRED FOOT	RIGHT

APPEARANCES	313
INTERCEPTIONS	262
GOALS	47
TACKLES	544
CLEARANCES	266
PASSES	18,243
PENALTIES SCORED	0
BLOCKS	29
AERIAL DUELS WON	42%
PASS COMPLETION	88.1%

MAJOR CLUB HONORS

⚽ Ligue 1: 2022, 2023, 2024, 2025, 2026 ⚽ Serie A: 2021 (Inter Milan) ⚽ UEFA Champions League: 2018 (R. Madrid), 2025, 2026 ⚽ FIFA World Club Cup: 2017, runner-up 2025, (R. Madrid) ⚽ Coupe de France: 2024, 2025

INTERNATIONAL HONORS

⚽ Africa Cup of Nations: 2025

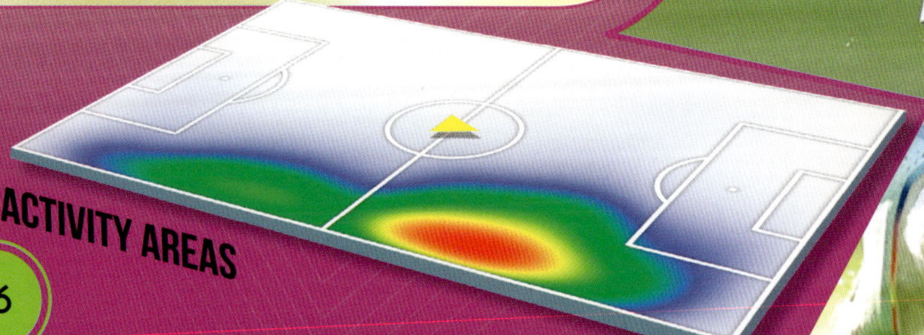

ACTIVITY AREAS

DEAN HUIJSEN

A towering young center-back, Huijsen rose quickly from Juventus to Bournemouth and Real Madrid. Born in the Netherlands but capped by Spain, he is strong in the air, calm on the ball, and dangerous in both penalty areas from set pieces and corners.

NATIONALITY
Spain

CURRENT CLUB
Real Madrid

24

DATE OF BIRTH	APR 14, 2005
POSITION	CENTER-BACK
HEIGHT	6 FT, 6 IN
PRO DEBUT	2023
PREFERRED FOOT	RIGHT

APPEARANCES 88

INTERCEPTIONS 91

GOALS 7

TACKLES 98

CLEARANCES 416

PASSES 4,659

PENALTIES SCORED 0

BLOCKS 58

AERIAL DUELS WON 58.9%

PASS COMPLETION 87.5%

MAJOR CLUB HONORS
- None to date

INTERNATIONAL HONORS
- UEFA Nations League: runner-up 2025

ACTIVITY AREAS

JOSHUA KIMMICH

NATIONALITY
Germany

CURRENT CLUB
Bayern Munich

A smart, versatile leader, Kimmich can control games from midfield or shine at right-back. For Bayern Munich, he uses his passing, tackling, and tireless running to set the tempo. For Germany, he has captained the team and shown his timing, crossing, and sharp reading of danger.

DATE OF BIRTH	FEB 8, 1995
POSITION	RIGHT-BACK
HEIGHT	5 FT, 10 IN
PRO DEBUT	2013
PREFERRED FOOT	RIGHT

APPEARANCES 439
INTERCEPTIONS 458
GOALS 43
TACKLES 639
CLEARANCES 369
PASSES 32,836
PENALTIES SCORED 2
BLOCKS 86
AERIAL DUELS WON 44.9%
PASS COMPLETION 90.6%

MAJOR CLUB HONORS
⚽ Bundesliga: 2016, 2017, 2018, 2019, 2020, 2021, 2022, 2023, 2025, 2026 ⚽ UEFA Champions League: 2020 ⚽ DFB-Pokal: 2016, 2019, 2020, TBC ⚽ FIFA Club World Cup: 2020

INTERNATIONAL HONORS
⚽ FIFA Confederations Cup: 2017

ACTIVITY AREAS

AYMERIC LAPORTE

Back in La Liga with Athletic Bilbao, Laporte brings strength and calm to the heart of defense. A Champions League winner with Manchester City and Euro 2024 winner with Spain, he reads danger well, wins headers, and starts attacks with precise passes from the back.

NATIONALITY
Spain

CURRENT CLUB
Athletic Bilbao

DATE OF BIRTH	MAY 27, 1994
POSITION	CENTRAL
HEIGHT	6 FT, 2 IN
PRO DEBUT	2011
PREFERRED FOOT	LEFT

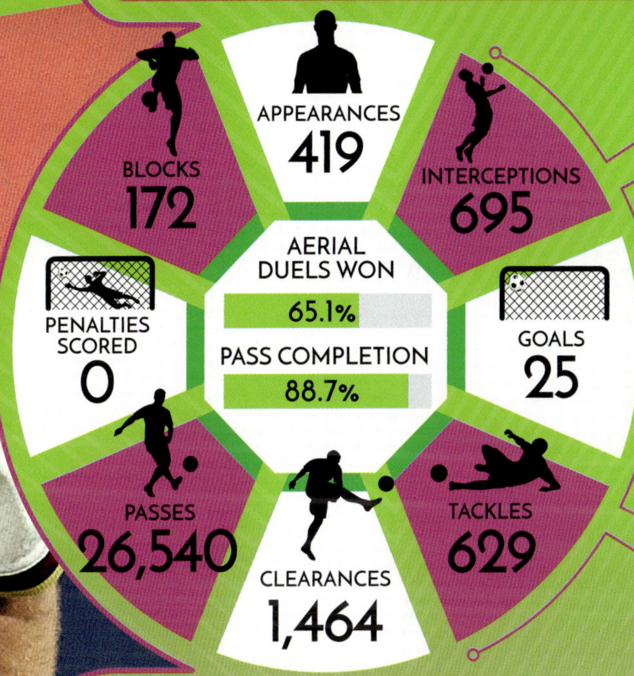

MAJOR CLUB HONORS

⚽ Premier League: 2018, 2019, 2021, 2022, 2023 (all Man. City) ⚽ UEFA Champions League: runner-up 2021, 2023 (all Man. City) ⚽ FA Cup: 2019, 2023 (all Man. City)

INTERNATIONAL HONORS

⚽ UEFA Nations League: runner-up 2021, 2023
⚽ UEFA European Championship: 2024

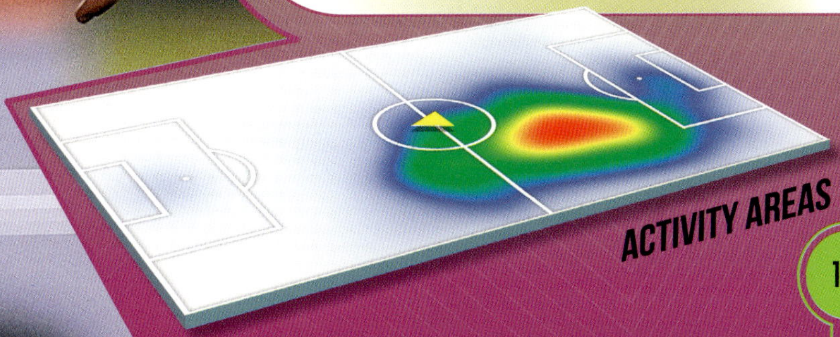

ACTIVITY AREAS

22

NATIONALITY
Italy

CURRENT CLUB
Napoli

GIOVANNI DI LORENZO

A strong and reliable right-back, Di Lorenzo captains Napoli and has helped them win two Serie A titles. He began his career as an attacking player, which shows when he drives forward from defense. Tough in tackles and strong in the air, he can also play at center-back when needed.

DATE OF BIRTH	AUG 4, 1993
POSITION	RIGHT-BACK
HEIGHT	6 FT
PRO DEBUT	2010
PREFERRED FOOT	BOTH

APPEARANCES 324
INTERCEPTIONS 265
GOALS 24
TACKLES 578
CLEARANCES 486
PASSES 18,335
PENALTIES SCORED 0
BLOCKS 99

AERIAL DUELS WON 52.9%
PASS COMPLETION 86.0%

MAJOR CLUB HONORS
- Serie A: 2023, 2025
- Coppa Italia: 2020

INTERNATIONAL HONORS
- UEFA European Championship: 2020 (2021)
- UEFA Nations League: third place 2021, 2023

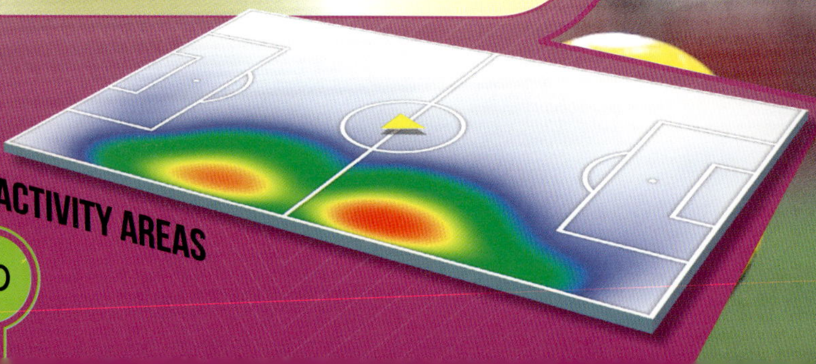
ACTIVITY AREAS

MARQUINHOS

A smart and calm center-back, Marquinhos captained PSG to its first Champions League title in 2025. Quick, agile, and sharp at reading danger, he can stop speedy forwards, make important interceptions, and guide the defense. With the ball, he can help launch attacks from deep.

NATIONALITY
Brazil

CURRENT CLUB
Paris Saint-Germain

DATE OF BIRTH	14 MAY, 1994
POSITION	CENTRAL
HEIGHT	6 FT
PRO DEBUT	2012
PREFERRED FOOT	RIGHT

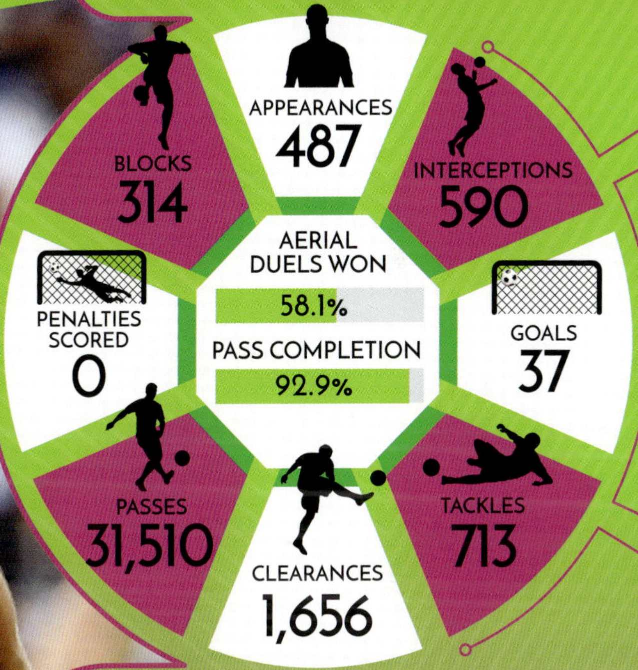

MAJOR CLUB HONORS

- Ligue 1: 2014, 2015, 2016, 2018, 2019, 2020, 2022, 2023, 2024, 2025, 2026
- UEFA Champions League: runner-up 2020, 2025, 2026
- FIFA World Club Cup: runner-up 2025
- Coupe de France: 2015, 2016, 2017, 2018, runner-up 2019, 2020, 2021, 2024, 2025

INTERNATIONAL HONORS

- Copa América: 2019, runner-up 2021
- Olympic Games: 2016

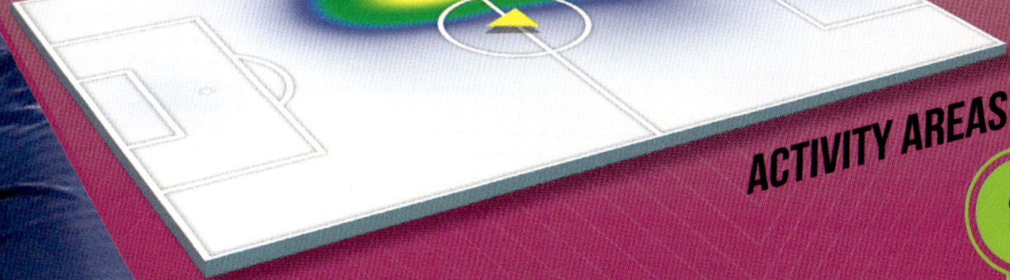

ACTIVITY AREAS

16

NATIONALITY
Argentina

CURRENT CLUB
Atlético Madrid

NAHUEL MOLINA

At his best with space to attack down the right, Molina is a fast, hard-working full-back or wing-back. A World Cup and Copa América winner with Argentina, he can race back to tackle, then surge forward to deliver dangerous passes and crosses.

DATE OF BIRTH	APR 6, 1998
POSITION	RIGHT-BACK
HEIGHT	5 FT, 9 IN
PRO DEBUT	2016
PREFERRED FOOT	RIGHT

APPEARANCES	222
INTERCEPTIONS	116
GOALS	18
TACKLES	315
CLEARANCES	266
PASSES	7,328
PENALTIES SCORED	0
BLOCKS	29
AERIAL DUELS WON	37.7%
PASS COMPLETION	78.6%

MAJOR CLUB HONORS
- None to date

INTERNATIONAL HONORS
- FIFA World Cup: 2022
- Copa América: 2021, 2024
- CONMEBOL—UEFA Cup of Champions: 2022

ACTIVITY AREAS

BENJAMIN PAVARD

A World Cup winner with France, Pavard brings experience and calm to defense. Comfortable at center-back or right-back, he times his tackles well and is strong in the air. He can also start attacks with sharp passes from deep, turning defense into attack.

NATIONALITY
France

CURRENT CLUB
Inter Milan (on Loan to Marseille)

28

DATE OF BIRTH	MAR 28, 1996
POSITION	CENTRAL
HEIGHT	6 FT, 1 IN
PRO DEBUT	2014
PREFERRED FOOT	RIGHT

APPEARANCES 328
INTERCEPTIONS 501
GOALS 13
TACKLES 452
CLEARANCES 966
PASSES 18,855
PENALTIES SCORED 0
BLOCKS 170
AERIAL DUELS WON 60.5%
PASS COMPLETION 88.3%

MAJOR CLUB HONORS
⚽ Serie A: 2024 ⚽ Bundesliga: 2020, 2021, 2022, 2023 (all B. Munich) ⚽ UEFA Champions League: 2020 (B. Munich), runner-up 2025 ⚽ FIFA Club World Cup: 2020 (B. Munich) ⚽ DFB-Pokal: 2020 (B. Munich)

INTERNATIONAL HONORS
⚽ FIFA World Cup: 2018, runner-up 2022
⚽ UEFA Nations League: 2021, third place 2025

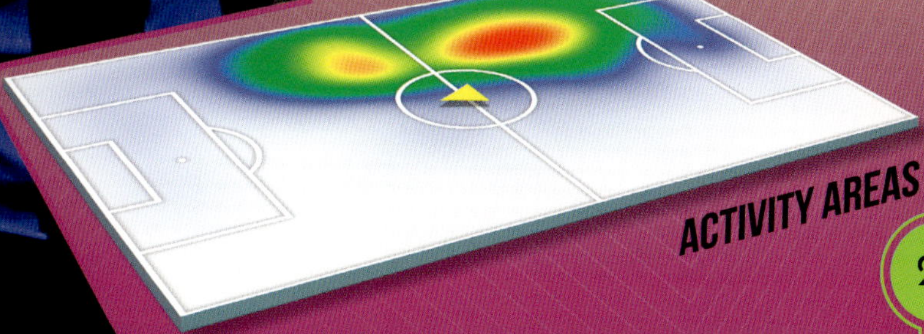

ACTIVITY AREAS

26

NATIONALITY
Scotland

CURRENT CLUB
To be confirmed

ANDREW ROBERTSON

A tireless left-back and Scotland captain, Robertson helped Liverpool win the Champions League and Premier League. Quick, tough, and full of energy, he can race down the flank, link with teammates, and whip dangerous crosses into the box. In 2026, he prepared to lead Scotland at the World Cup.

DATE OF BIRTH	MAR 11, 1994
POSITION	LEFT-BACK
HEIGHT	5 FT, 10 IN
PRO DEBUT	2012
PREFERRED FOOT	LEFT

APPEARANCES 403
INTERCEPTIONS 344
GOALS 14
TACKLES 567
CLEARANCES 669
PASSES 22,046
PENALTIES SCORED 0
BLOCKS 80
AERIAL DUELS WON 50.7%
PASS COMPLETION 84.1%

MAJOR CLUB HONORS
⚽ Premier League: 2020, 2025 ⚽ UEFA Champions League: 2019 ⚽ FIFA World Club Cup: 2019 ⚽ UEFA Super Cup: 2019 ⚽ FA Cup: 2022

INTERNATIONAL HONORS
⚽ None to date

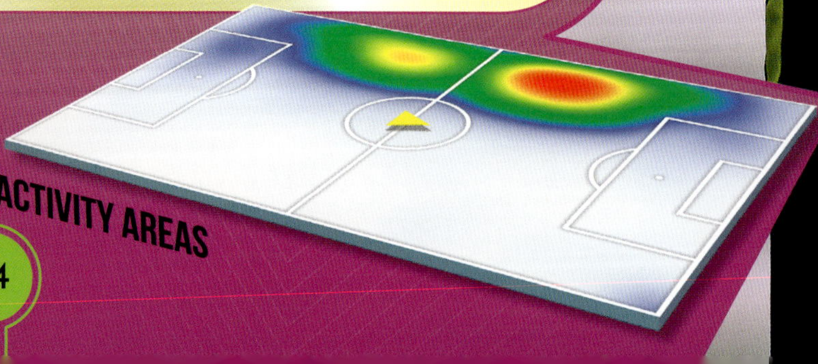

ACTIVITY AREAS

ANTONEE ROBINSON

A fast, energetic left-back, Robinson is a key player for Fulham and the USA. Nicknamed "Jedi," he reads danger quickly, makes sharp interceptions, and races forward to join attacks. In 2025, his crosses and passes made him one of the Premier League's top assist-making defenders.

NATIONALITY
USA

CURRENT CLUB
Fulham

DATE OF BIRTH	AUG 8, 1997
POSITION	LEFT-BACK
HEIGHT	6 FT
PRO DEBUT	2015
PREFERRED FOOT	LEFT

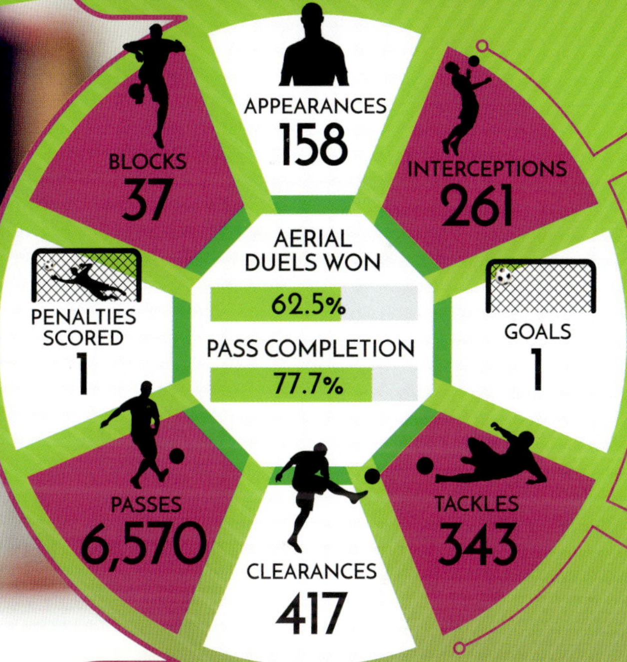

MAJOR CLUB HONORS
- EFL Championship: 2022

INTERNATIONAL HONORS
- CONCACAF Nations League: 2020, 2023, 2024

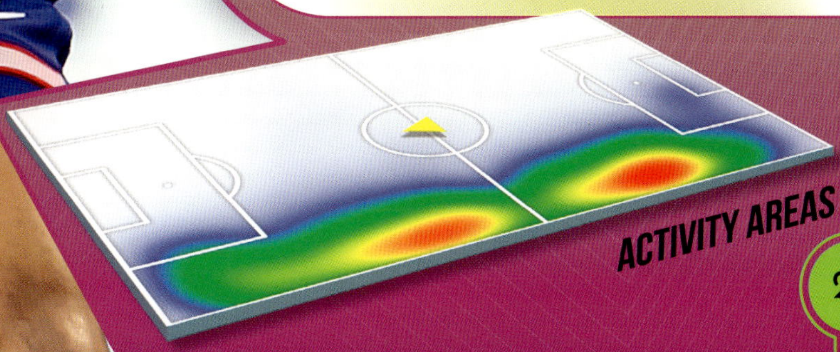

ANTONIO RÜDIGER

22

NATIONALITY
Germany

CURRENT CLUB
Real Madrid

A Champions League winner with Chelsea and Real Madrid, Rüdiger brings power, presence, and energy to defense. Usually a center-back, he can also play at full-back if needed. Tall, quick, and strong, he wins headers, times tackles well, and is hard to get past.

DATE OF BIRTH	MAR 3, 1993
POSITION	CENTRAL
HEIGHT	6 FT, 3 IN
PRO DEBUT	2011
PREFERRED FOOT	RIGHT

APPEARANCES 465
INTERCEPTIONS 404
GOALS 20
TACKLES 562
CLEARANCES 1,524
PASSES 27,115
PENALTIES SCORED 0
BLOCKS 200

AERIAL DUELS WON 59.6%
PASS COMPLETION 88.4%

MAJOR CLUB HONORS

⚽ La Liga: 2024 ⚽ UEFA Champions League: 2021 (Chelsea), 2024 ⚽ FIFA World Club Cup: 2021 (Chelsea), 2022 ⚽ UEFA Europa League 2019 (Chelsea) ⚽ UEFA Super Cup: 2021 (Chelsea), 2022, 2024 ⚽ FA Cup: 2018 (Chelsea) ⚽ Copa del Rey: 2023

INTERNATIONAL HONORS

⚽ FIFA Confederations Cup: 2017

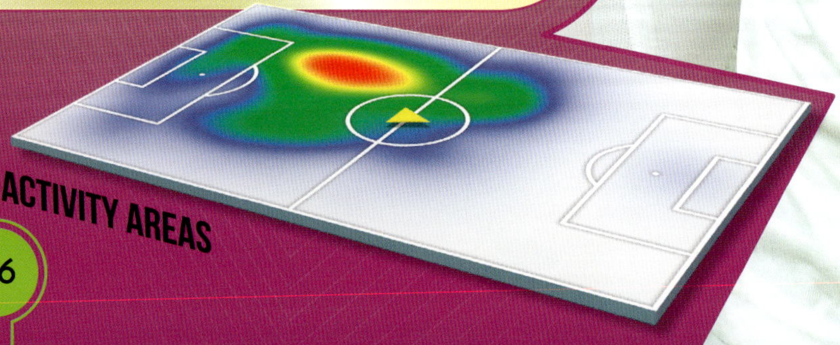

ACTIVITY AREAS

WILLIAM SALIBA

A calm and classy center-back, Saliba has become one of Arsenal and France's most important defenders. Strong, quick, and hard to beat, he reads danger early and times his tackles well. In 2025–26, he helped champions Arsenal build one of the Premier League's toughest defenses.

NATIONALITY
France

CURRENT CLUB
Arsenal

DATE OF BIRTH	MAR 24, 2001
POSITION	CENTER-BACK
HEIGHT	6 FT, 4 IN
PRO DEBUT	2018
PREFERRED FOOT	RIGHT

APPEARANCES	267
INTERCEPTIONS	257
GOALS	9
TACKLES	349
CLEARANCES	808
PASSES	18,663
PENALTIES SCORED	0
BLOCKS	111
AERIAL DUELS WON	58.9%
PASS COMPLETION	92.1%

MAJOR CLUB HONORS
⚽ Premier League: 2026 ⚽ UEFA Champions League: runner-up 2026 ⚽ Coupe de France: runner-up 2020 (PSG)

INTERNATIONAL HONORS
⚽ FIFA World Cup: runners-up 2022

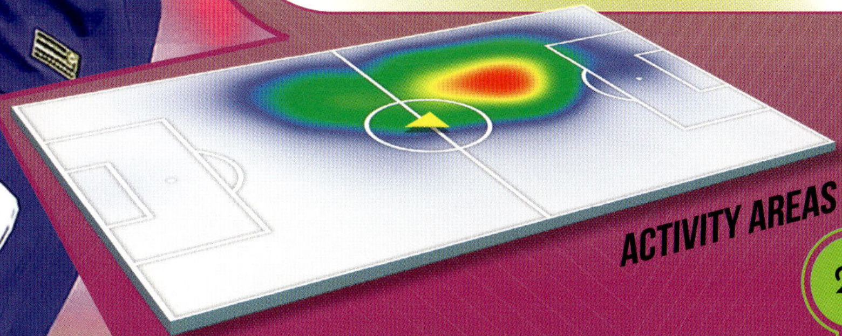

ACTIVITY AREAS

42

NATIONALITY
Italy

CURRENT CLUB
Atalanta

GEORGIO SCALVINI

A tall and talented center-back, Scalvini is strong in the air and calm in the tackle. He helped Atalanta win the Europa League in 2024, but a serious knee injury ruled him out of EURO 2024 with Italy. Now rebuilding his career, he remains one of Italy's most exciting young defenders.

DATE OF BIRTH	DEC 11, 2003
POSITION	CENTER-BACK
HEIGHT	6 FT, 4 IN
PRO DEBUT	2021
PREFERRED FOOT	RIGHT

APPEARANCES 127
INTERCEPTIONS 197
GOALS 8
TACKLES 211
CLEARANCES 241
PASSES 5,294
PENALTIES SCORED 0
BLOCKS 47

AERIAL DUELS WON 60.7%
PASS COMPLETION 83.2%

MAJOR CLUB HONORS
- UEFA Europa League: 2024

INTERNATIONAL HONORS
- None to date

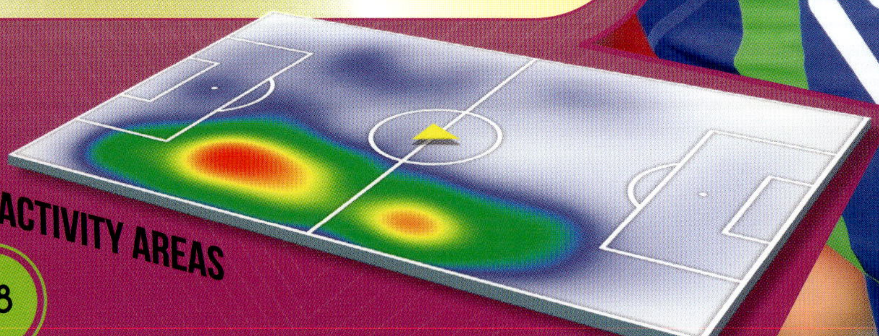

ACTIVITY AREAS

THIAGO SILVA

Still going strong in his forties, Silva remains one of soccer's classiest center-backs. A Champions League winner with Chelsea and former captain of Brazil and PSG, he uses calmness, leadership, and brilliant positioning to read danger and make important clearances.

NATIONALITY
Brazil

CURRENT CLUB
Porto

DATE OF BIRTH	SEP 22, 1984
POSITION	CENTER-BACK
HEIGHT	6 FT
PRO DEBUT	2002
PREFERRED FOOT	RIGHT

APPEARANCES 591

INTERCEPTIONS 1,095

GOALS 29

TACKLES 777

CLEARANCES 2,881

PASSES 37,806

PENALTIES SCORED 0

BLOCKS 411

AERIAL DUELS WON 71.1%

PASS COMPLETION 92.6%

MAJOR CLUB HONORS

⚽ UEFA Champions League: 2021 (Chelsea), runner-up 2020 (PSG) ⚽ UEFA Super Cup: 2021 (Chelsea) ⚽ FIFA Club World Cup: 2021 (Chelsea) ⚽ Serie A: 2011 (AC Milan) ⚽ Ligue 1: 2013-2020 (PSG) ⚽ Coupe de France: 2015-18, 2020 (all PSG) ⚽ FA Cup: 2022 (Chelsea)

INTERNATIONAL HONORS

⚽ FIFA Confederations Cup; 2013
⚽ Copa América: 2019, runner-up 2021
⚽ Olympic Games: silver medal 2012, bronze medal 2008

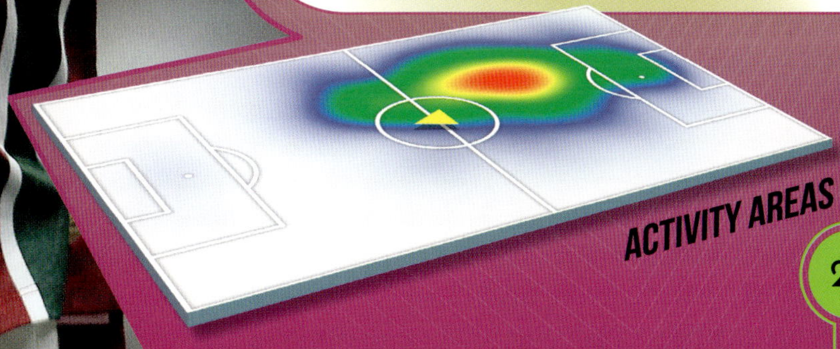

ACTIVITY AREAS

MILAN ŠKRINIAR

37

NATIONALITY
Slovakia

CURRENT CLUB
Fenerbahce (Turkey)

Now at Fenerbahçe, Škriniar is a strong and fearless center-back who captains Slovakia. He wins headers, makes tough tackles. and stays calm when attackers close him down. He can pick out smart passes and help his team build from the back.

DATE OF BIRTH	FEB 11, 1995
POSITION	CENTER-BACK
HEIGHT	6 FT, 2 IN
PRO DEBUT	2012
PREFERRED FOOT	RIGHT

APPEARANCES 353

INTERCEPTIONS 306

GOALS 17

TACKLES 558

CLEARANCES 1,222

PASSES 22,181

PENALTIES SCORED 0

BLOCKS 227

AERIAL DUELS WON 52.6%

PASS COMPLETION 92.4%

MAJOR CLUB HONORS

⚽ Ligue 1: 2024, 2025 (PSG) ⚽ Serie A: 2021 (Inter Milan) ⚽ UEFA Champions League: runner-up 2023 (Inter Milan), 2025 ⚽ UEFA Europa League: runner-up 2020 (Inter Milan) ⚽ Coupe de France: 2024, 2025 (all PSG) ⚽ Coppa Italia: 2022, 2023 (Inter Milan)

INTERNATIONAL HONORS

⚽ King's Cup: 2018

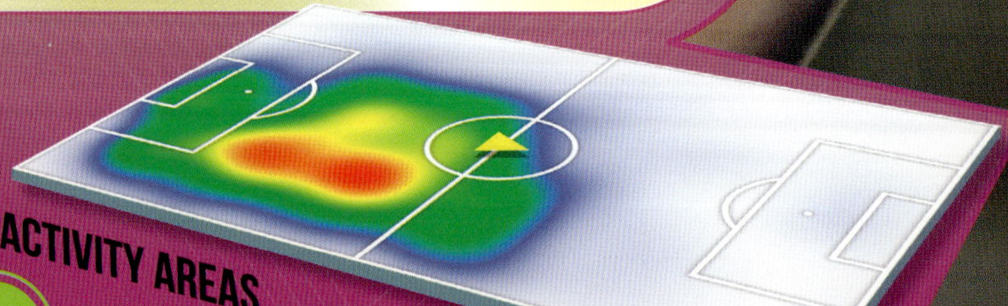

ACTIVITY AREAS

DAYOT UPAMECANO

A key center-back for Bayern Munich and France, Upamecano signed a new Bayern deal in 2026. Quick, strong, and calm on the ball, he can stop danger, carry the ball out from defense and start attacks with sharp passes from the back.

NATIONALITY
France

CURRENT CLUB
Bayern Munich

2

DATE OF BIRTH	OC 27, 1998
POSITION	CENTER-BACK
HEIGHT	6 FT, 1 IN
PRO DEBUT	2015
PREFERRED FOOT	RIGHT

APPEARANCES	325
INTERCEPTIONS	453
GOALS	10
TACKLES	633
CLEARANCES	902
PASSES	22,298
PENALTIES SCORED	0
BLOCKS	117
AERIAL DUELS WON	60.1%
PASS COMPLETION	89.5%

MAJOR CLUB HONORS

- Bundesliga: 2022, 2023, 2025, 2026
- DFB-Pokal: TBC
- DFL Supercup: 2021

INTERNATIONAL HONORS

- UEFA Nations League: 2021
- FIFA World Cup: runner-up 2022

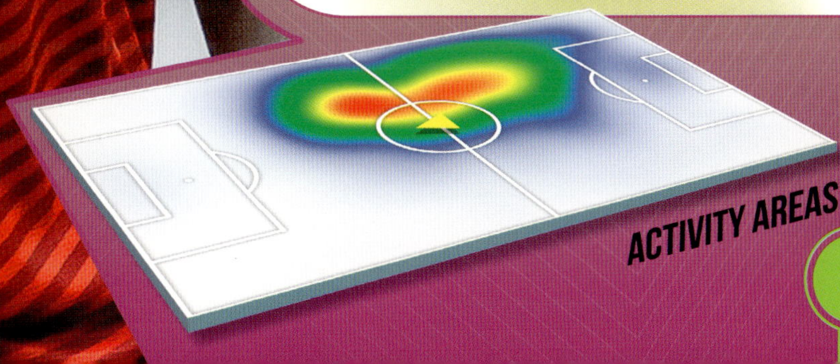

ACTIVITY AREAS

MIDFIELDERS

Midfielders are the heartbeat of a team. They link defense and attack, helping their team win the ball, keep possession, and create chances. Because the ball often passes through midfield, these players need energy, skill, and quick thinking. Defensive midfielders protect the back line and break up attacks. Wide midfielders race down the wings and cross into the box. Central midfielders pass, tackle, and join attacks. Playmakers use vision and skill to unlock defenses with smart passes. The best midfielders can change a game without even scoring.

WHAT DO THE STATS MEAN?

ASSISTS

A pass, cross, or header to a teammate who then scores counts as an assist. This stat also includes a deflected shot that is converted by a teammate.

SHOTS

Any deliberate strike on goal counts as a shot. The strike does not have to be on target or force a save from the keeper.

CHANCES CREATED

Any pass that results in a shot at goal (whether or not the goal is scored) is regarded as a chance created.

TACKLES

This is the number of times the player has challenged and dispossessed the opposition without committing a foul.

DRIBBLES

This is the number of times the player has gone past an opponent while running with the ball.

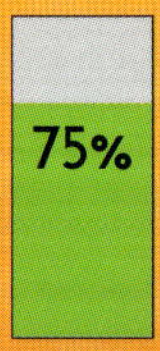

SUCCESSFUL PASSES

This shows as a percentage how successful the midfielder is at finding teammates with passes, whether over 15 or 200 feet.

Did you know?

Midfielders tend to do the most running in a game. "Box to box" central midfielders will cover between 6 and 7.5 miles (more than a quarter of a marathon) over 90 minutes.

5

NATIONALITY
England

CURRENT CLUB
Real Madrid

JUDE BELLINGHAM

A Real Madrid and England star, Bellingham is a midfielder who can do almost everything. He tackles, drives forward, creates chances, and scores important goals. After helping Real Madrid win the Champions League in 2024, he was voted England's best player for 2024–25.

DATE OF BIRTH	JUN 29, 2003
POSITION	CENTRAL
HEIGHT	6 FT, 1 IN
PRO DEBUT	2019
PREFERRED FOOT	RIGHT

APPEARANCES 244
DRIBBLES 706
GOALS 64
TACKLES 469
CHANCES CREATED 309
SHOTS 429
PENALTIES SCORED 3
ASSISTS 50
PASSES 11,127
SUCCESSFUL PASSES 86.6%

MAJOR CLUB HONORS

- La Liga: 2024
- UEFA Champions League: 2024
- Bundesliga: runner-up 2023 (Borussia Dortmund)
- DFB-Pokal: 2021 (Borussia Dortmund)

INTERNATIONAL HONORS

- UEFA European Championship: runner-up 2020 (2021), runner-up 2024

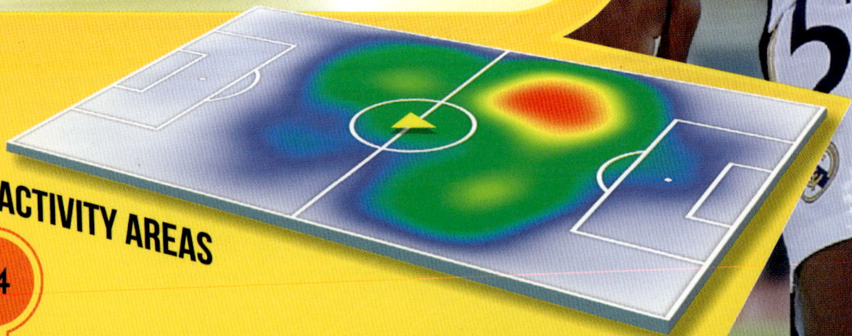

ACTIVITY AREAS

KEVIN DE BRUYNE

A modern midfield great, De Bruyne joined Napoli in 2025 after a trophy-filled decade at Manchester City. Brilliant with both feet, he can split defenses with smart passes, whip in dangerous crosses, and fire unstoppable shots from long range.

NATIONALITY
Belgium

CURRENT CLUB
Napoli

DATE OF BIRTH	JUN 28, 1991
POSITION	ATTACKING
HEIGHT	5 FT, 11 IN
PRO DEBUT	2008
PREFERRED FOOT	RIGHT

APPEARANCES 484

DRIBBLES 1,307

GOALS 121

TACKLES 547

CHANCES CREATED 1,354

SHOTS 1,135

PENALTIES SCORED 8

ASSISTS 188

PASSES 22,682

SUCCESSFUL PASSES 80.9%

MAJOR CLUB HONORS

⚽ Premier League: 2018, 2019, 2021, 2022, 2023, 2024 (all Manchester City) ⚽ UEFA Champions League: runner-up 2021, 2023 (all Man City) ⚽ FA Cup: 2019, 2023 (all Manchester City) ⚽ DFB-Pokal: 2015 (VfL Wolfsburg)

INTERNATIONAL HONORS

⚽ FIFA World Cup: third place 2018

ACTIVITY AREAS

EDUARDO CAMAVINGA

NATIONALITY
France

CURRENT CLUB
Real Madrid

A brilliant and versatile Real Madrid midfielder, Camavinga can also shine at left-back. He reads danger quickly, wins tackles, and makes sharp interceptions before launching attacks with smart passes. Full of energy and confidence, he can cover huge spaces across the field.

DATE OF BIRTH	NOV 10, 2002
POSITION	DEFENSIVE
HEIGHT	6 FT, 1 IN
PRO DEBUT	2019
PREFERRED FOOT	LEFT

- APPEARANCES 274
- DRIBBLES 378
- GOALS 7
- TACKLES 663
- CHANCES CREATED 147
- SHOTS 139
- PENALTIES SCORED 0
- ASSISTS 14
- PASSES 10,142
- SUCCESSFUL PASSES 90.1%

MAJOR CLUB HONORS

⚽ La Liga: 2022, 2024 ⚽ UEFA Champions League: 2022, 2024 ⚽ Copa del Rey: 2023 ⚽ FIFA Club World Cup: 2022 ⚽ UEFA Super Cup: 2022, 2024 ⚽ FIFA Intercontinental Cup: 2024

INTERNATIONAL HONORS

⚽ FIFA World Cup: runner-up 2022

ACTIVITY AREAS

EMRE CAN

A strong and versatile leader, Can captains Borussia Dortmund and can play in midfield or defense. He uses his strength to win tackles, then looks for smart passes to start attacks. His experience helps him organize teammates and protect the back line.

NATIONALITY
Germany

CURRENT CLUB
Borussia Dortmund

23

DATE OF BIRTH	JAN 12, 1994
POSITION	CENTRAL
HEIGHT	6 FT, 1 IN
PRO DEBUT	2011
PREFERRED FOOT	RIGHT

APPEARANCES 427

DRIBBLES 655

GOALS 40

TACKLES 900

CHANCES CREATED 245

SHOTS 346

PENALTIES SCORED 15

ASSISTS 21

PASSES 21,563

SUCCESSFUL PASSES 85.6%

MAJOR CLUB HONORS

⚽ Bundesliga: 2013 (B. Munich), runner-up 2023, runner-up 2026 ⚽ UEFA Champions League: 2013 (B. Munich), runner-up 2018 (Liverpool), runner-up 2024 ⚽ UEFA Europa League: runner-up 2016 (Liverpool) ⚽ Serie A: 2019, 2020 (Juventus) ⚽ DFB-Pokal: 2013 (B. Munich) 2021

INTERNATIONAL HONORS

⚽ FIFA Confederations Cup: 2017

ACTIVITY AREAS

NATIONALITY
Canada

CURRENT CLUB
Bayern Munich

ALPHONSO DAVIES

A flying left-back with incredible pace, Davies is one of Canada's greatest soccer players and a star for Bayern Munich. He can race down the left, dribble past opponents, and whip dangerous crosses into the box. After injury setbacks, he returned to help Bayern win the 2025–26 Bundesliga title.

DATE OF BIRTH	NOV 2, 2000
POSITION	LEFT WING
HEIGHT	6 FT
PRO DEBUT	2016
PREFERRED FOOT	LEFT

APPEARANCES 291
DRIBBLES 1,261
GOALS 21
TACKLES 478
CHANCES CREATED 321
SHOTS 185
PENALTIES SCORED 0
ASSISTS 43
PASSES 11,844
SUCCESSFUL PASSES 87.3%

MAJOR CLUB HONORS

⚽ Bundesliga: 2019, 2020, 2021, 2022, 2023, 2025, 2026 ⚽ UEFA Champions League: 2020 ⚽ FIFA Club World Cup 2020 ⚽ UEFA Super Cup: 2020 ⚽ DFB-Pokal: 2019, 2020, 2026

INTERNATIONAL HONORS

⚽ None to date

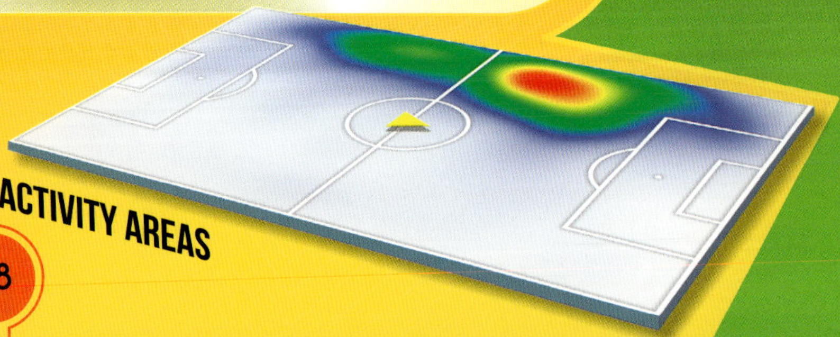

ACTIVITY AREAS

OUSMANE DEMBÉLÉ

A thrilling attacking midfielder, Dembélé can play wide, through the middle or as a false nine. His speed, dribbling, and two-footed skill make him a nightmare for defenders. After a brilliant 2025–26 season with PSG, he became one of Europe's most feared attackers.

NATIONALITY
France

CURRENT CLUB
Paris Saint-Germain

10

DATE OF BIRTH	MAY 15, 1997
POSITION	WINGER/FORWARD
HEIGHT	5 FT, 10
PRO DEBUT	2014
PREFERRED FOOT	BOTH

APPEARANCES 352
DRIBBLES 1,559
GOALS 106
TACKLES 237
CHANCES CREATED 636
SHOTS 738
PENALTIES SCORED 7
ASSISTS 94
PASSES 10,789
SUCCESSFUL PASSES 80.5%

MAJOR CLUB HONORS

⚽ Ligue 1: 2024, 2025, 2026 ⚽ UEFA Champions League: 2025, 2026 ⚽ La Liga: 2018, 2019, 2023 (all Barcelona) ⚽ Coupe de France: 2024, 2025 ⚽ FIFA World Club Cup: runner-up 2025 ⚽ Copa del Rey: 2018, 2021 (all Barcelona) ⚽ DFB Pokal: 2017 (Borussia Dortmund)

INTERNATIONAL HONORS

⚽ FIFA World Cup: 2018, runner-up 2022
⚽ UEFA Nations League third place: 2025

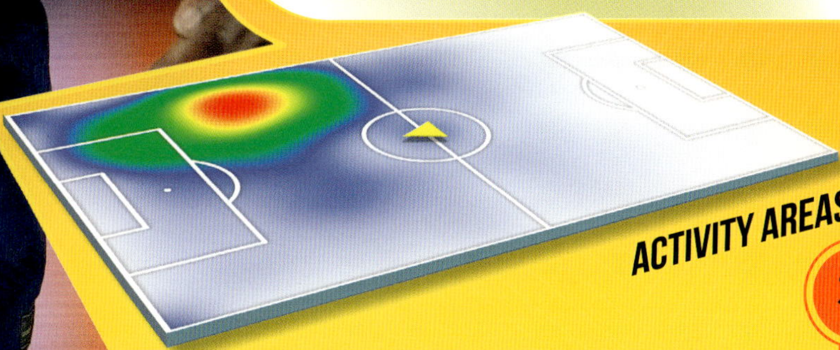

ACTIVITY AREAS

BRUNO FERNANDES

NATIONALITY
Portugal

CURRENT CLUB
Manchester United

A brilliant creator and Manchester United captain, Fernandes can play in central or attacking midfield. He spots passes others miss, fires shots from long range, and stays cool from penalties and free kicks. In 2025–26, he broke the Premier League single-season assists record.

DATE OF BIRTH	SEP 8, 1994
POSITION	ATTACKING
HEIGHT	5 FT, 10 IN
PRO DEBUT	2012
PREFERRED FOOT	RIGHT

APPEARANCES 515

ASSISTS 142

DRIBBLES 914

PASSES 24,273

SUCCESSFUL PASSES 77.9%

PENALTIES SCORED 54

GOALS 159

SHOTS 1,350

CHANCES CREATED 1,285

TACKLES 861

*Excludes data from Portuguese Premeira League

MAJOR CLUB HONORS

⚽ UEFA Europa League: runner-up 2021, runner-up 2025 ⚽ Taça de Portugal: 2019 (Sporting CP) ⚽ Taça de Liga: 2018, 2019 (Sporting CP) ⚽ FA Cup: runner-up 2023, 2024

INTERNATIONAL HONORS

⚽ UEFA Nations League: 2019, 2025

ACTIVITY AREAS

ENZO FERNÁNDEZ

A World Cup winner with Argentina, Fernández gives Chelsea drive and control in midfield. He can break up attacks, spot space quickly, and send smart passes forward. For club and country, his energy, vision, and big-game experience make him a key figure in the middle.

NATIONALITY
Argentina

CURRENT CLUB
Chelsea

DATE OF BIRTH	JAN 17, 2001
POSITION	CENTRAL
HEIGHT	5 FT, 10 IN
PRO DEBUT	2019
PREFERRED FOOT	RIGHT

APPEARANCES	221
DRIBBLES	283
GOALS	36
TACKLES	413
CHANCES CREATED	350
SHOTS	357
PENALTIES SCORED	9
ASSISTS	41
PASSES	13,370
SUCCESSFUL PASSES	85.8%

MAJOR CLUB HONORS

UEFA Conference League: 2025 • EFL Cup: 2025 • FIFA World Club Cup: 2025 • Argentina Primera División: 2021 (River Plate)

INTERNATIONAL HONORS

- FIFA World Cup: 2022
- Copa América: 2024

ACTIVITY AREAS

YOUSSOUF FOFANA

A strong box-to-box midfielder, Fofana brings power and energy to AC Milan and France. He can break up attacks, win tackles, and drive forward with the ball. After joining Milan from Monaco, he helped add bite and balance to their midfield.

19

NATIONALITY
France

CURRENT CLUB
AC Milan

DATE OF BIRTH	JAN 10, 1999
POSITION	CENTRAL
HEIGHT	6 FT, 1 IN
PRO DEBUT	2017
PREFERRED FOOT	RIGHT

APPEARANCES	264
DRIBBLES	472
GOALS	13
TACKLES	505
CHANCES CREATED	216
SHOTS	305
PENALTIES SCORED	0
ASSISTS	27
PASSES	10,614
SUCCESSFUL PASSES	83.0%

MAJOR CLUB HONORS
- Coupe De La Ligue: 2019 (Strasbourg)
- Coupe de France: runner-up 2022 (Monaco)

INTERNATIONAL HONORS
- FIFA World Cup: runner-up 2022

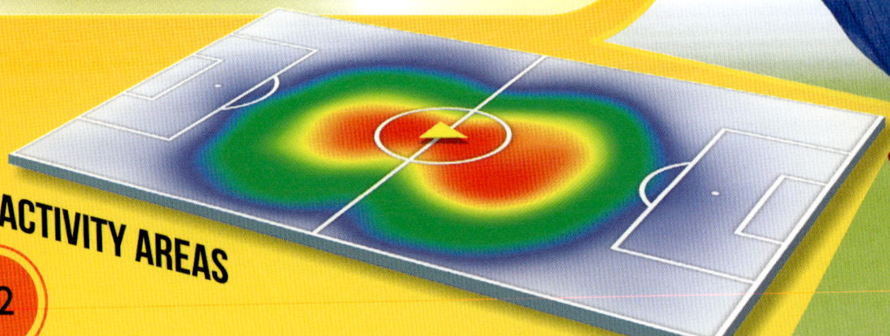

ACTIVITY AREAS

GAVI

A fearless Barcelona midfielder, Gavi plays with bite, skill, and huge energy. He can win tackles, dribble through pressure, and move the ball quickly with smart passes. After another knee setback in 2025, he returned in 2026 to boost Barcelona and Spain.

NATIONALITY
Spain

CURRENT CLUB
Barcelona

DATE OF BIRTH	AUG 5, 2004
POSITION	CENTRAL
HEIGHT	5 FT, 9 IN
PRO DEBUT	2021
PREFERRED FOOT	RIGHT

APPEARANCES 151
ASSISTS 12
DRIBBLES 238
PASSES 4,957
SUCCESSFUL PASSES 89.6%
PENALTIES SCORED 0
GOALS 7
SHOTS 92
CHANCES CREATED 111
TACKLES 216

NEW ENTRY!

MAJOR CLUB HONORS
- La Liga: 2023, 2025, 2026
- Copa del Rey: 2025

INTERNATIONAL HONORS
- UEFA Nations League: 2024, runner-up 2025

ACTIVITY AREAS

21

NATIONALITY
Netherlands

CURRENT CLUB
Barcelona

FRENKIE DE JONG

A smooth and smart Barcelona midfielder, De Jong controls games with quick feet, sharp passing, and calm movement under pressure. He can glide away from opponents and carry the ball into attack. In 2025, he signed a new Barcelona contract until 2029.

DATE OF BIRTH	MAY 12, 1997
POSITION	CENTRAL
HEIGHT	5 FT, 11 IN
PRO DEBUT	2015
PREFERRED FOOT	RIGHT

APPEARANCES 336

DRIBBLES 532

GOALS 20

TACKLES 468

CHANCES CREATED 382

SHOTS 143

PENALTIES SCORED 0

ASSISTS 34

PASSES 20,795

SUCCESSFUL PASSES 92.1%

MAJOR CLUB HONORS

⚽ La Liga: 2023, 2025, 2026 ⚽ UEFA Europa League: runner-up 2017 (Ajax) ⚽ Copa del Rey: 2021, 2025 ⚽ Eredivisie: 2019 (Ajax) ⚽ KNVB Cup: 2019 (Ajax)

INTERNATIONAL HONORS

⚽ UEFA Nations League: runner-up: 2019

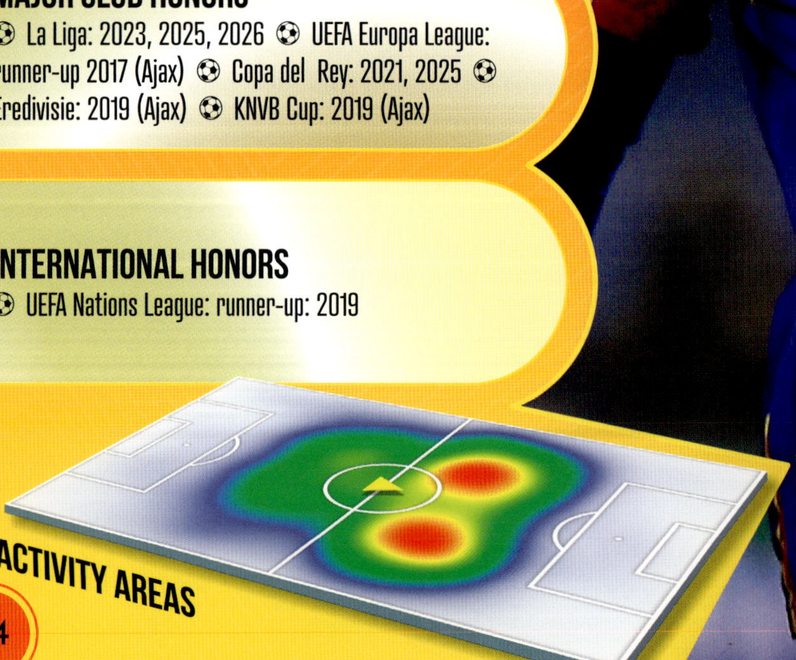

ACTIVITY AREAS

MANUEL LOCATELLI

A smart Juventus captain, Locatelli protects the defense and keeps the ball moving in midfield. He reads danger early, wins tackles, and uses his passing range to launch attacks from deep. In 2026, he signed a new Juventus contract until 2030.

NATIONALITY
Italy

CURRENT CLUB
Juventus

5

DATE OF BIRTH	JAN 5, 1998
POSITION	DEFENSIVE
HEIGHT	6 FT, 1 IN
PRO DEBUT	2016
PREFERRED FOOT	RIGHT

APPEARANCES 363
DRIBBLES 334
GOALS 16
TACKLES 730
CHANCES CREATED 323
SHOTS 320
PENALTIES SCORED 4
ASSISTS 25
PASSES 20,143
SUCCESSFUL PASSES 86.7%

MAJOR CLUB HONORS
- Coppa Italia: 2024

INTERNATIONAL HONORS
- UEFA European Championship: 2020
- UEFA Nations League: third place 2021

NEW ENTRY!

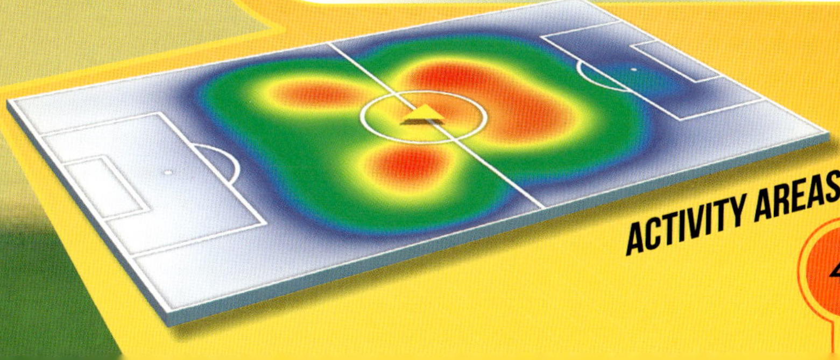
ACTIVITY AREAS

ALEXIS MAC ALLISTER

NATIONALITY
Argentina

CURRENT CLUB
Liverpool

A World Cup winner with Argentina, Mac Allister brings calm and control to Liverpool's midfield. He can play deep, attack from central areas, and spot passes into dangerous spaces. He also works hard without the ball, breaking up attacks before moving his team forward.

DATE OF BIRTH	DEC 24, 1998
POSITION	CENTRAL
HEIGHT	5 FT, 9 IN
PRO DEBUT	2016
PREFERRED FOOT	RIGHT

APPEARANCES	229
DRIBBLES	274
GOALS	34
TACKLES	462
CHANCES CREATED	260
SHOTS	346
PENALTIES SCORED	10
ASSISTS	22
PASSES	9,160
SUCCESSFUL PASSES	86.5%

MAJOR CLUB HONORS

- Premier League: 2025
- EFL Cup: 2024, runner-up 2025
- Primera División: 2020 (Boca Juniors)

INTERNATIONAL HONORS

- FIFA World Cup: 2022
- Copa América: 2024
- CONMEBOL—UEFA Cup of Champions: 2022

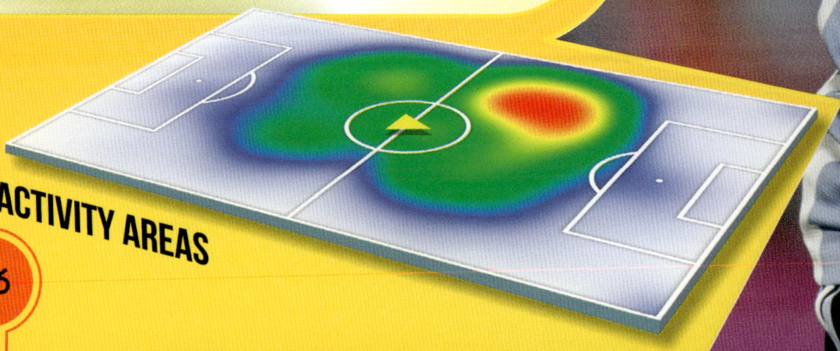

ACTIVITY AREAS

WESTON MCKENNIE

A tough and energetic midfielder, McKennie brings bite, running power, and attacking threat for Juventus and the USA. He can win tackles, break up play, and make late runs into the box. Strong in the air and full of fight, he gives his team danger from midfield.

NATIONALITY
USA

CURRENT CLUB
Juventus

16

DATE OF BIRTH	AUG 28, 1998
POSITION	CENTRAL
HEIGHT	6 FT, 1 IN
PRO DEBUT	2017
PREFERRED FOOT	RIGHT

APPEARANCES 313
DRIBBLES 348
GOALS 31
TACKLES 393
CHANCES CREATED 283
SHOTS 266
PENALTIES SCORED 0
ASSISTS 26
PASSES 8,775
SUCCESSFUL PASSES 80.4%

MAJOR CLUB HONORS
- Coppa Italia: 202, 2024

INTERNATIONAL HONORS
- CONCACAF Nations League: 2020, 2023, 2024
- CONCACAF Gold Cup: runner-up: 2019

ACTIVITY AREAS

NATIONALITY
Scotland

CURRENT CLUB
Napoli

SCOTT MCTOMINEY

A powerful midfielder, McTominay found a successful new role after joining Napoli. Pushed farther forward, he became a real goal threat, using his strength, timing, and dangerous runs into the penalty area. He also brings aerial power and tough tackling to Scotland's midfield.

DATE OF BIRTH	DEC 8, 1996
POSITION	ATTACKING
HEIGHT	6 FT, 3 IN
PRO DEBUT	2017
PREFERRED FOOT	RIGHT

APPEARANCES 295
DRIBBLES 405
GOALS 48
TACKLES 393
CHANCES CREATED 154
SHOTS 391
PENALTIES SCORED 0
ASSISTS 13
PASSES 9,445
SUCCESSFUL PASSES 85.6%

MAJOR CLUB HONORS

⚽ Serie A: 2025 ⚽ UEFA Europa League: runner-up 2021 (Manchester United) ⚽ FA Cup: 2024 (Manchester United)

INTERNATIONAL HONORS

⚽ None to date

ACTIVITY AREAS

NEW ENTRY!

LUKA MODRIĆ

A top player for more than 20 years (13 seasons with Real Madrid) and a Ballon d'Or winner in 2018, Luka Modrić is still capable of moments of magic on the field. He has a great soccer brain, can deliver long and short passes with both feet, and can strike powerful long-range shots, especially free kicks.

NATIONALITY
Croatia

CURRENT CLUB
AC Milan

DATE OF BIRTH	SEP 9, 1985
POSITION	ATTACKING
HEIGHT	5 FT, 8 IN
PRO DEBUT	2003
PREFERRED FOOT	RIGHT

APPEARANCES	723
DRIBBLES	1,551
GOALS	57
TACKLES	895
CHANCES CREATED	1,108
SHOTS	789
PENALTIES SCORED	6
ASSISTS	102
PASSES	39,649
SUCCESSFUL PASSES	89.2%

MAJOR CLUB HONORS

⚽ La Liga: 2017, 2020, 2022 (all Real Madrid) ⚽ UEFA Champions League: 2014, 2016, 2017, 2018, 2022, 2024 (all R. Mad.) ⚽ UEFA Super Cup: 2014, 2016, 2017, 2022 (all R. Mad.) ⚽ FIFA Club World Cup: 2014, 2016, 2017, 2018, 2022 (all R. Mad.) ⚽ Copa del Rey: 2014, 2023 (all R. Mad.)

INTERNATIONAL HONORS

⚽ FIFA World Cup: runner-up 2018, third place 2022
⚽ UEFA Nations League: runner-up 2023

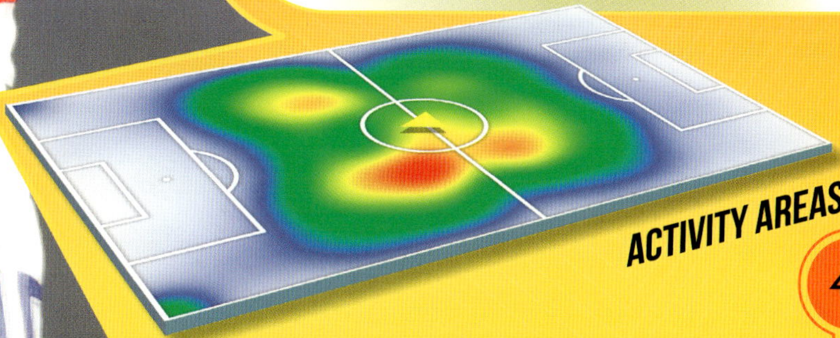

ACTIVITY AREAS

25

NATIONALITY
Germany

CURRENT CLUB
Bayern Munich

JAMAL MUSIALA

A dazzling Bayern Munich and Germany attacker, Musiala can play in midfield, or farther forward. His quick feet, sharp turns, and fearless dribbling make him a nightmare to tackle. After fighting back from a serious 2025 injury, he returned in 2026 with his magic still intact.

DATE OF BIRTH	FEB 26, 2003
POSITION	ATTACKING/WINGER
HEIGHT	6 FT
PRO DEBUT	2020
PREFERRED FOOT	RIGHT

APPEARANCES	210
DRIBBLES	871
GOALS	60
TACKLES	248
CHANCES CREATED	255
SHOTS	382
PENALTIES SCORED	2
ASSISTS	35
PASSES	5,498
SUCCESSFUL PASSES	84.6%

MAJOR CLUB HONORS

⚽ Bundesliga: 2020, 2021, 2022, 2023, 2025, 2026 ⚽ DFB-Pokal: 2026 ⚽ UEFA Champions League: 2020 ⚽ FIFA Club World Cup: 2020

INTERNATIONAL HONORS

⚽ None to date

ACTIVITY AREAS

COLE PALMER

Palmer can play in midfield or across the front line. Left-footed but dangerous with either foot, he dribbles past defenders, spots smart passes, and stays calm from penalties and free kicks. Even after injury setbacks, his talent still makes him Chelsea's danger man.

NATIONALITY
England

CURRENT CLUB
Chelsea

DATE OF BIRTH	MAY 6, 2002
POSITION	ATTACKING
HEIGHT	6 FT, 1 IN
PRO DEBUT	2020
PREFERRED FOOT	LEFT

APPEARANCES 140
DRIBBLES 363
GOALS 53
TACKLES 106
CHANCES CREATED 219
SHOTS 364
PENALTIES SCORED 18
ASSISTS 28
PASSES 4,321
SUCCESSFUL PASSES 84.4%

MAJOR CLUB HONORS
⚽ Premier League: 2023 (Man. City) ⚽ UEFA Champions League: 2023 (Man. City) ⚽ FIFA World Club Cup: 2025 ⚽ UEFA Conference League: 2025 ⚽ FA Cup: 2023 (Man. City), runner-up 2026

INTERNATIONAL HONORS
⚽ UEFA European Championship: runner-up 2024

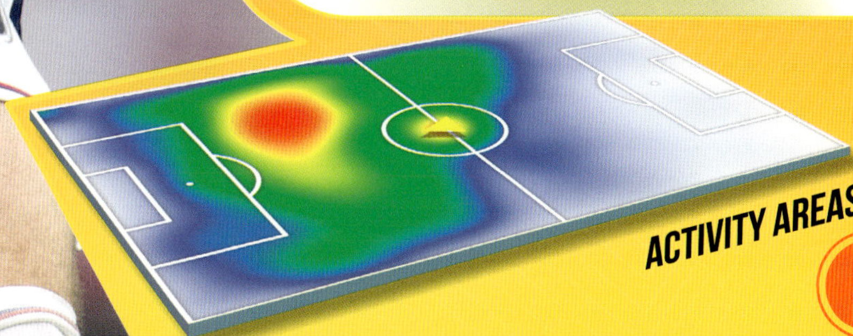

ACTIVITY AREAS

NATIONALITY
USA

CURRENT CLUB
AC Milan

CHRISTIAN PULISIC

A quick and smart attacker, Pulisic can play wide or through the middle for AC Milan and the USA. He can burst past defenders, cut inside to shoot, or make dangerous runs into the box. In 2026, he helped lead the USA at a World Cup partly hosted on home soil.

DATE OF BIRTH	SEP 18, 1998
POSITION	RIGHT
HEIGHT	5 FT 10 IN
PRO DEBUT	2016
PREFERRED FOOT	BOTH

APPEARANCES 365
DRIBBLES 1,328
GOALS 78
TACKLES 326
CHANCES CREATED 403
SHOTS 539
PENALTIES SCORED 3
ASSISTS 56
PASSES 8,355
SUCCESSFUL PASSES 81.4%

MAJOR CLUB HONORS

- UEFA Champions League: 2021 (Chelsea)
- UEFA Super Cup: 2021 (Chelsea)
- FIFA Club World Cup: 2021 (Chelsea)
- DFB-Pokal: 2017 (Borussia Dortmund)

INTERNATIONAL HONORS

- CONCACAF Nations League: 2020, 2023, 2024
- ONCACAF Gold Cup: runner-up 2019

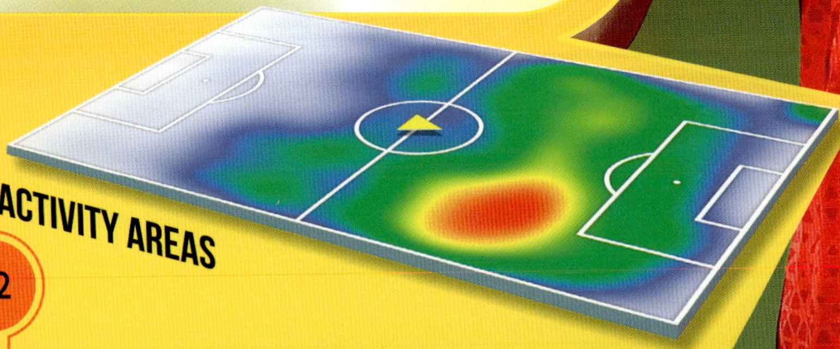

ACTIVITY AREAS

DECLAN RICE

A powerful Arsenal and England midfielder, Rice has become much more than a defensive shield. He can win tackles, drive forward, cross dangerously, and strike from distance. In 2025–26, his energy and tactical intelligence helped Arsenal win the Premier League title.

NATIONALITY
England

CURRENT CLUB
Arsenal

41

DATE OF BIRTH	JAN 14, 1999
POSITION	DEFENSIVE
HEIGHT	6 FT, 2 IN
PRO DEBUT	2015
PREFERRED FOOT	RIGHT

APPEARANCES 370
DRIBBLES 452
GOALS 34
TACKLES 768
CHANCES CREATED 343
SHOTS 345
PENALTIES SCORED 1
ASSISTS 36
PASSES 18,187
SUCCESSFUL PASSES 88.6%

MAJOR CLUB HONORS

- Premier League: runner-up 2024, runner-up 2025, 2026
- UEFA Champions League: runner-up 2026
- UEFA Europa Conference League: 2023 (West Ham Utd)

INTERNATIONAL HONORS

- UEFA European Championship: runner-up 2020 (2021), runner-up 2024
- UEFA Nations League: (third place) 2019

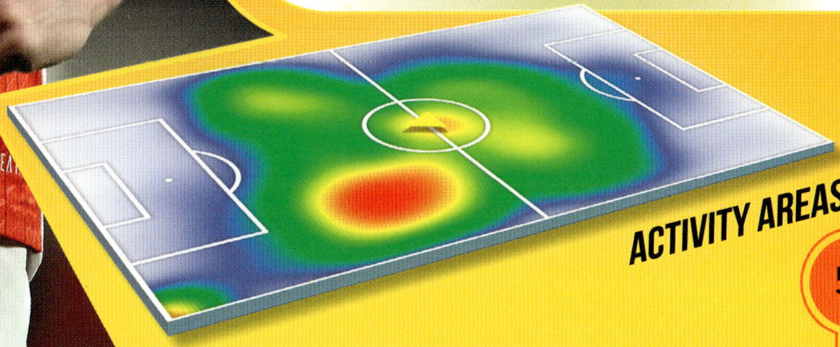
ACTIVITY AREAS

NATIONALITY
England

CURRENT CLUB
Arsenal

BUKAYO SAKA

A brilliant right-sided midfielder, Saka is one of Arsenal and England's biggest stars. He uses quick feet, strength, and calm decision-making to beat defenders, create chances, and score important goals. Even after injury setbacks, he remains a constant danger on the right.

DATE OF BIRTH	SEP 5, 2001
POSITION	WINGER
HEIGHT	5 FT, 10 IN
PRO DEBUT	2018
PREFERRED FOOT	LEFT

APPEARANCES	280
DRIBBLES	893
GOALS	78
TACKLES	360
CHANCES CREATED	491
SHOTS	609
PENALTIES SCORED	14
ASSISTS	66
PASSES	7,961
SUCCESSFUL PASSES	81.5%

MAJOR CLUB HONORS

⚽ Premier League: runner-up 2023, runner-up 2024, runner-up 2025, 2026 ⚽ UEFA Champions League: runner-up 2026 ⚽ FA Cup: 2020 ⚽ UEFA Europa League: runner-up 2019

INTERNATIONAL HONORS

⚽ UEFA European Championship: runner-up 2020 (2021), runner-up 2024

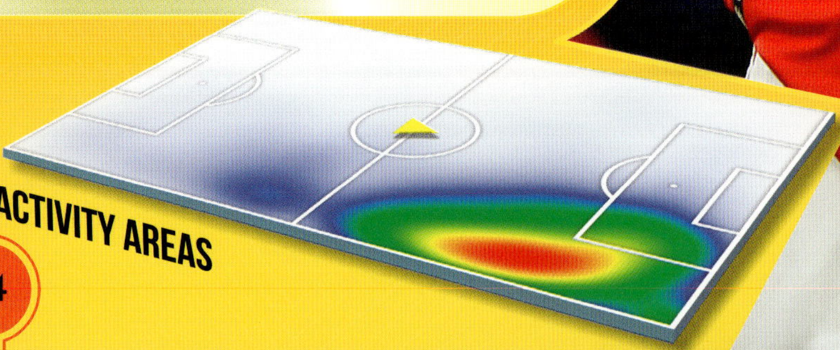

ACTIVITY AREAS

LEROY SANÉ

A lightning-fast winger for Galatasaray and Germany, Sané is dangerous on either flank. Left-footed but often flying down the right, he can beat defenders with pace, close control, and sharp dribbling. After five seasons at Bayern Munich, he began a new challenge in Turkey.

NATIONALITY
Germany

CURRENT CLUB
Galatasaray (Turkey)

DATE OF BIRTH	JAN 11, 1996
POSITION	WINGER
HEIGHT	6 FT
PRO DEBUT	2014
PREFERRED FOOT	LEFT

APPEARANCES 412
DRIBBLES 1,832
GOALS 107
TACKLES 432
CHANCES CREATED 572
SHOTS 849
PENALTIES SCORED 0
ASSISTS 97
PASSES 11,770
SUCCESSFUL PASSES 83.5%

MAJOR CLUB HONORS
⚽ Bundesliga: 2021, 2022, 2023, 2025 (all B. Munich) ⚽ FIFA Club World Cup: 2020 2021 (all B. Munich) ⚽ UEFA Super Cup: 2020 (B. Munich) ⚽ Premier League: 2018, 2019 (all Man. City) ⚽ FA Cup: 2019 (Man. City) ⚽ Süper Lig: 2026

INTERNATIONAL HONORS
⚽ FIFA Confederations Cup: 2017

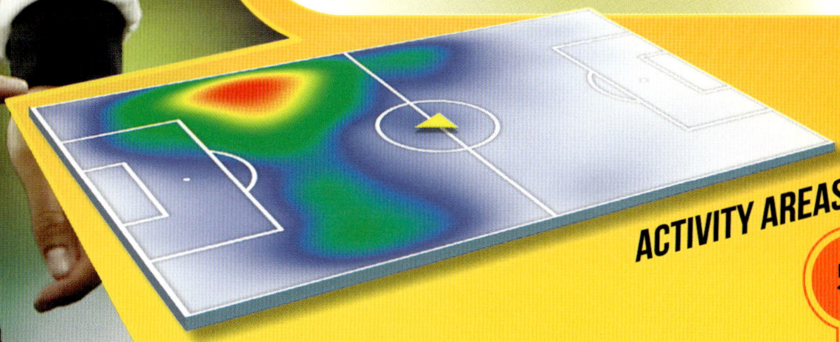

ACTIVITY AREAS

NATIONALITY
Belgium

CURRENT CLUB
Girona

AXEL WITSEL

A vastly experienced Belgian midfielder, Witsel brings calm, strength, and leadership to Girona. Once a speedy winger, he has become a smart defensive midfielder who can also play at center-back. He wins the ball, keeps possession, and helps his team build attacks with smart passes.

DATE OF BIRTH	JAN 12, 1989
POSITION	DEFENSIVE
HEIGHT	6 FT, 1 IN
PRO DEBUT	2006
PREFERRED FOOT	RIGHT

APPEARANCES	372
DRIBBLES	244
GOALS	25
TACKLES	483
CHANCES CREATED	134
SHOTS	233
PENALTIES SCORED	2
ASSISTS	14
PASSES	17,589
SUCCESSFUL PASSES	91.8%

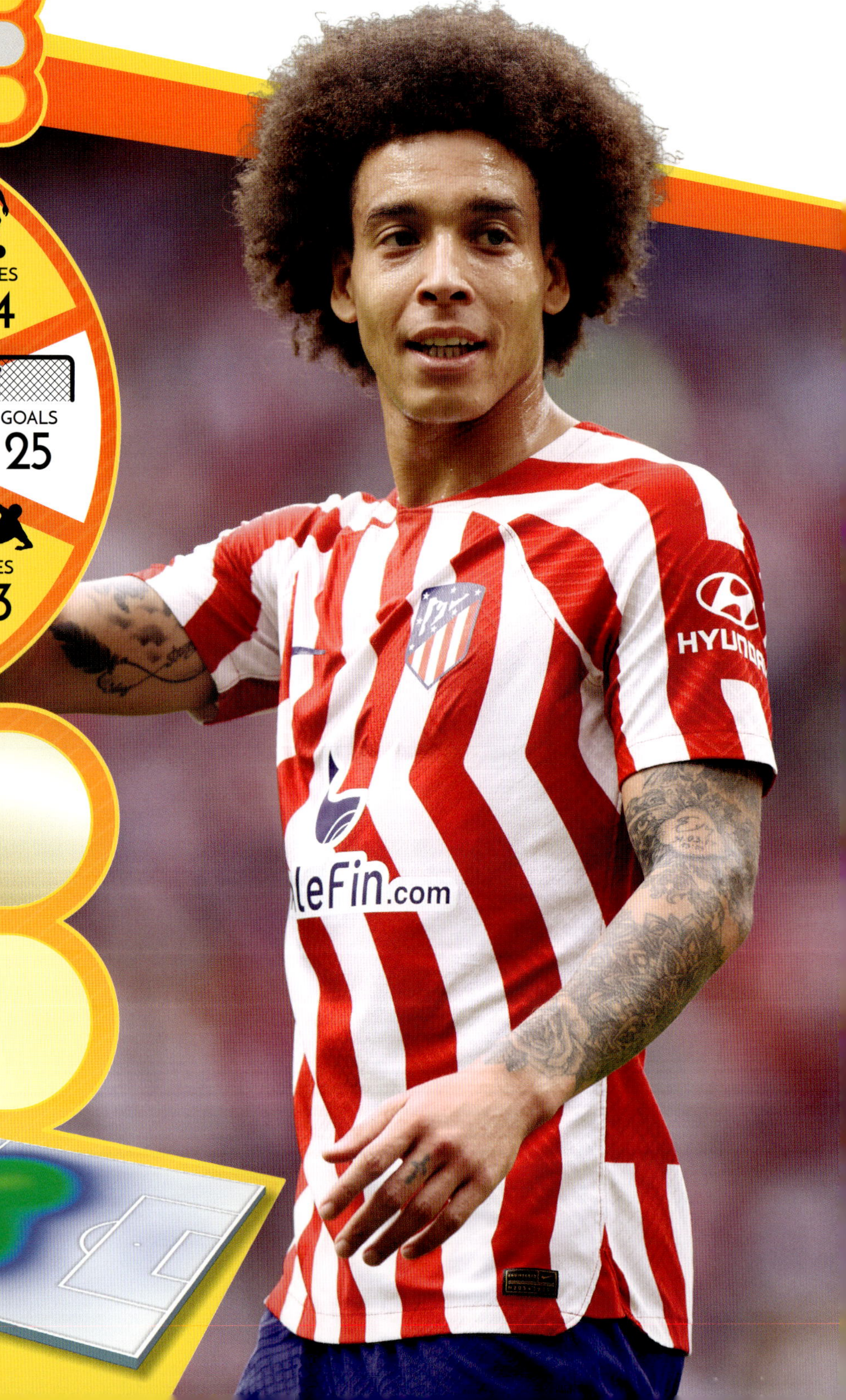

MAJOR CLUB HONORS

- DFL-Pokal: 2021 (Borussia Dortmund)

INTERNATIONAL HONORS

- FIFA World Cup: third place 2018

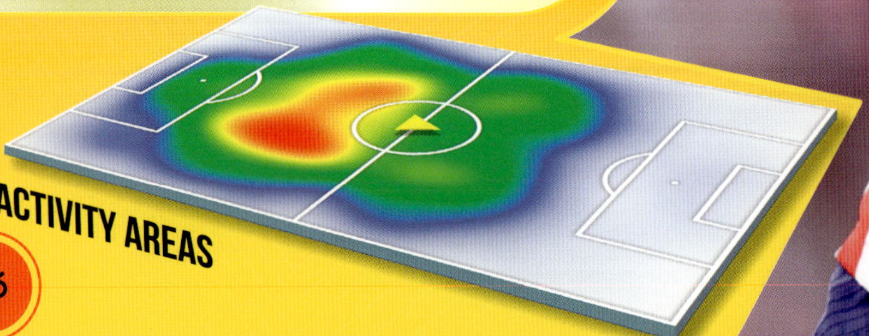

ACTIVITY AREAS

GRANIT XHAKA

A tough and smart midfielder, Xhaka brings leadership, control, and steel to the team. He reads danger, wins tackles, and keeps the ball moving with accurate passes. After starring on Bayer Leverkusen's unbeaten Bundesliga-winning team, he returned to the Premier League with Sunderland.

NATIONALITY
Switzerland

CURRENT CLUB
Sunderland

DATE OF BIRTH	SEP 27, 1992
POSITION	DEFENSIVE
HEIGHT	6 FT, 1 IN
PRO DEBUT	2010
PREFERRED FOOT	LEFT

APPEARANCES 528

DRIBBLES 513

GOALS 35

TACKLES 915

CHANCES CREATED 536

SHOTS 553

PENALTIES SCORED 1

ASSISTS 47

PASSES 36,268

SUCCESSFUL PASSES 87.8%

MAJOR CLUB HONORS

⚽ Bundesliga: 2024 (Bayer Leverkusen) ⚽ UEFA Europa League: runner-up 2019 (Arsenal), runner-up 2024 (Bayer Leverkusen) ⚽ DFB-Pokal: 2024 (Bayer Leverkusen) ⚽ FA Cup: 2017, 2020 (Arsenal) ⚽ Swiss Super League: 2011, 2012 (all Basel)

INTERNATIONAL HONORS

⚽ None to date

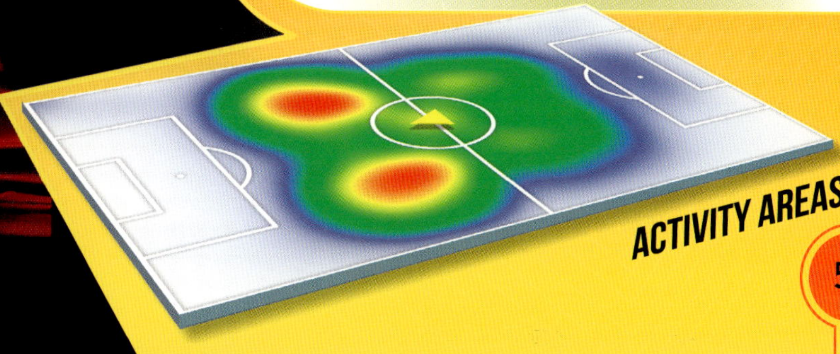

ACTIVITY AREAS

FORWARDS

The forwards are a team's frontline attackers and the chief goal-scorers. They are also the team's most celebrated players. Whether it is the smaller, quicker player, such as Neymar and Mohamed Salah, or the bigger, more physical attacker, such as Erling Haaland and Romelu Lukaku, strikers have perfected the art of finding the back of the net on a regular basis. Aside from scoring lots of goals, the world's best strikers are also effective at creating chances for their teammates.

WHAT DO THE STATS MEAN?

GOALS

This is the total number of goals a striker has scored. The figure spans across all the top clubs the player has represented so far in their career.

CONVERSION RATE

The percentage shows how good the player is at taking their chance in front of goal. If a player scores two goals from four shots, their conversion rate is 50 percent.

ASSISTS

A pass, cross, or header to a teammate who then scores counts as an assist. This stat also includes a deflected shot that is immediately converted by a teammate.

MINUTES PER GOAL

This is the average length of time it takes for the player to score. It is calculated across all the minutes the player has played in their career at top level.

Did you know?

A perfect hat-trick is one where the player scores one goal with his right foot, another with his left foot, and a third with his head. It does not matter in which order the goals come.

7

NATIONALITY
Canada

CURRENT CLUB
Juventus

JONATHAN DAVID

A sharp and speedy striker, David is one of Canada's biggest stars and now leads the line for Juventus. He finds pockets of space, links play with smart passes, and finishes coolly in the box. In 2026, he carried Canada's hopes at a home World Cup.

DATE OF BIRTH	JAN 14, 2000
POSITION	SECOND STRIKER
HEIGHT	5 FT, 10 IN
PRO DEBUT	2018
PREFERRED FOOT	BOTH

GOALS 111
PENALTIES SCORED 24
ASSISTS 24
GOALS RIGHT 66
SHOTS 516
HEADED GOALS 8
HAT-TRICKS 3
GOALS LEFT 37
APPEARANCES 263
SHOT CONVERSION 21.5%
MINUTES PER GOAL 170

MAJOR CLUB HONORS
- Ligue 1: 2021 (Lille)

INTERNATIONAL HONORS
- None to date

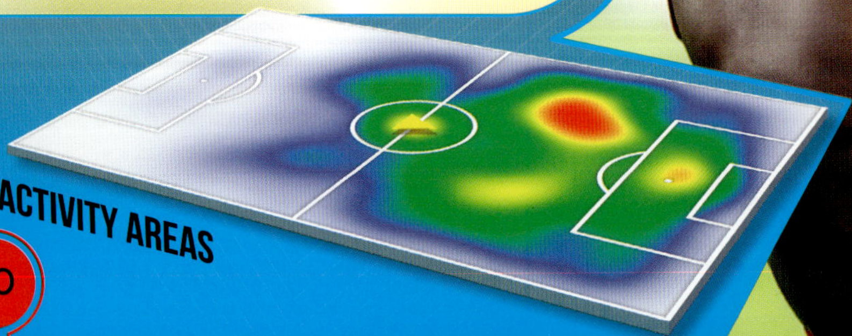

ACTIVITY AREAS

MEMPHIS DEPAY

A bold and skillful forward, Memphis can play from the left or through the middle. He dribbles with power, takes on defenders, and attacks the box with confidence. Now at Corinthians, he remains a major Netherlands star and their all-time leading scorer.

NATIONALITY
Netherlands

CURRENT CLUB
Corinthians (Brazil)

DATE OF BIRTH	FEB 13, 1994
POSITION	SECOND STRIKER
HEIGHT	5 FT, 10 IN
PRO DEBUT	2011
PREFERRED FOOT	RIGHT

GOALS	158
PENALTIES SCORED	24
ASSISTS	76
GOALS RIGHT	126
SHOTS	1,208
HEADED GOALS	7
HAT-TRICKS	3
GOALS LEFT	25
APPEARANCES	423
SHOT CONVERSION	13.1%
MINUTES PER GOAL	175

MAJOR CLUB HONORS

⚽ Copa de Brasil: 2025 ⚽ Supercopa do Brasil: 2026 ⚽ La Liga: 2023 (Barcelona) ⚽ UEFA Europe League: 2017 (Man. United ⚽ FA Cup: 2016 (Man. United ⚽ Eredivisie: 2015 (PSV Eindhoven) ⚽ KNVB Cup: 2012 (PSVEindhoven) ⚽ Coupe de La Ligue: runner-up 2020 (Lyon)

INTERNATIONAL HONORS

⚽ FIFA World Cup: third place 2014

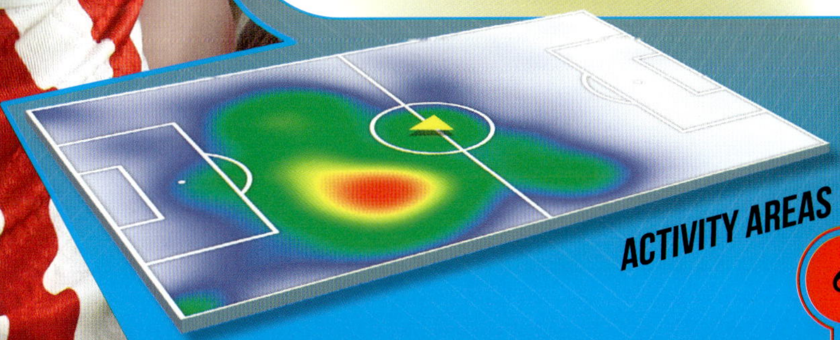

ACTIVITY AREAS

79

NATIONALITY
Portugal

CURRENT CLUB
Al-Nassr (S. Arabia)

JOÃO FÉLIX

A skillful Portuguese forward, João Félix loves to drift into pockets of space between defenders. He can play as a second striker or wide attacker, using quick feet, smart passes, and smart movement to create chances. In 2026, he joined Portugal's World Cup squad.

DATE OF BIRTH	NOV 10, 1999
POSITION	FORWARD
HEIGHT	5 FT, 11 IN
PRO DEBUT	2018
PREFERRED FOOT	RIGHT

GOALS 71
PENALTIES SCORED 4
ASSISTS 28
GOALS RIGHT 51
SHOTS 521
HEADED GOALS 8
HAT-TRICKS 1
GOALS LEFT 12
APPEARANCES 249

SHOT CONVERSION 13.6%
MINUTES PER GOAL 200

MAJOR CLUB HONORS
⚽ FIFA World Club Cup: 2025 ⚽ Saudi Pro League: 2026 ⚽ UEFA Conference League: 2025 ⚽ La Liga: 2021 (Atlético Madrid) ⚽ Primeira Liga: 2019 (Benfica)

INTERNATIONAL HONORS
⚽ UEFA Nations League: 2019, 2025

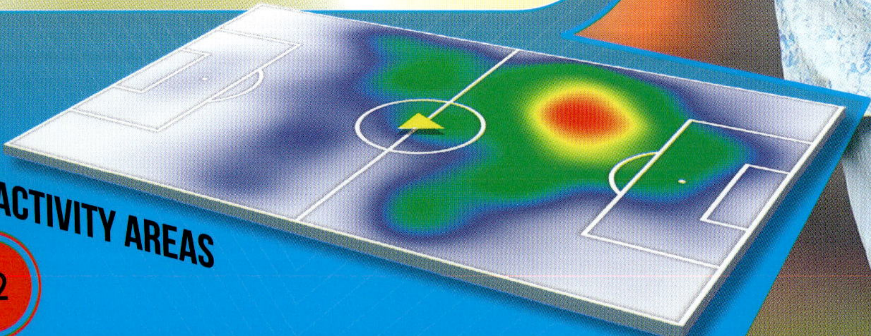

ACTIVITY AREAS

PHIL FODEN

A gifted attacker, Phil Foden can play wide, centrally, or just behind the striker. His first touch, balance, and close control help him wriggle away from defenders, while his left foot can create or score goals. After a difficult 2025–26 season, he is eager to bounce back.

NATIONALITY
England

CURRENT CLUB
Manchester City

DATE OF BIRTH	MAY 28, 2000
POSITION	SECOND STRIKER
HEIGHT	5 FT, 7 IN
PRO DEBUT	2016
PREFERRED FOOT	LEFT

GOALS 91
PENALTIES SCORED 0
ASSISTS 47
APPEARANCES 298
SHOT CONVERSION 15.9%
MINUTES PER GOAL 202
GOALS LEFT 70
GOALS RIGHT 16
HAT-TRICKS 3
HEADED GOALS 5
SHOTS 573

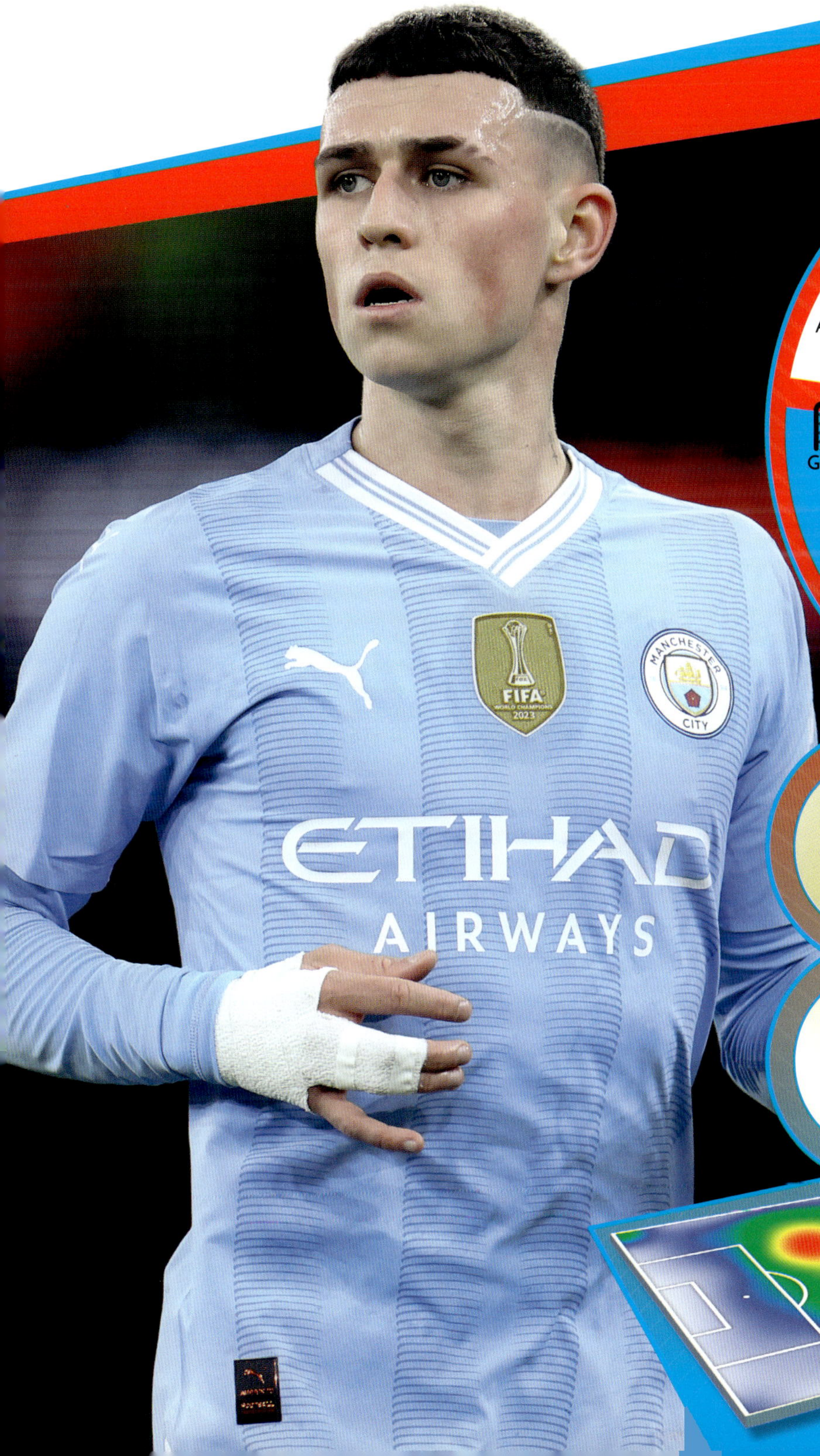

MAJOR CLUB HONORS

⚽ Premier League: 2018, 2019, 2021, 2022, 2023, 2024 ⚽ UEFA Champions League: 2023, runners-up 2021 ⚽ UEFA Super Cup: 2023 ⚽ FIFA Club World Cup: 2023 ⚽ FA Cup: 2019, 2023, runner-up 2024, 2026

INTERNATIONAL HONORS

⚽ UEFA European Championship: runner-up 2020, 2024

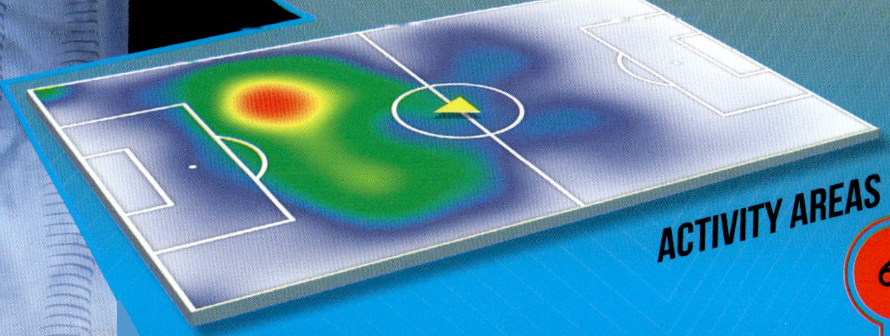

ACTIVITY AREAS

OLIVIER GIROUD

NATIONALITY
France

CURRENT CLUB
Lille

A smart and powerful striker, Giroud gives Lille experience, strength, and cool finishing. France's all-time leading scorer, he is much more than a target man. He can hold the ball up, link play with smart passes, and attack crosses with amazing headers.

DATE OF BIRTH	SEP 30, 1986
POSITION	STRIKER
HEIGHT	6 FT, 4 IN
PRO DEBUT	2005
PREFERRED FOOT	LEFT

GOALS	216
PENALTIES SCORED	27
ASSISTS	73
GOALS RIGHT	20
SHOTS	1,355
HEADED GOALS	64
HAT-TRICKS	7
GOALS LEFT	131
APPEARANCES	585
SHOT CONVERSION	15.9%
MINUTES PER GOAL	171

MAJOR CLUB HONORS

⚽ Serie A: 2022 (AC Milan) ⚽ UEFA Champions League: 2021 (Chelsea) ⚽ UEFA Europa League: 2019 (Chelsea) ⚽ Ligue 1: 2012 (Montpellier) ⚽ US Open Cup: 2024 ⚽ FA Cup: 2014, 2015, 2017 (all Arsenal), 2018 (Chelsea) 2017 (Arsenal), 2018 (Chelsea)

INTERNATIONAL HONORS

- ⚽ FIFA World Cup 2018, runner-up 2022
- ⚽ UEFA European Championship: runner-up 2016

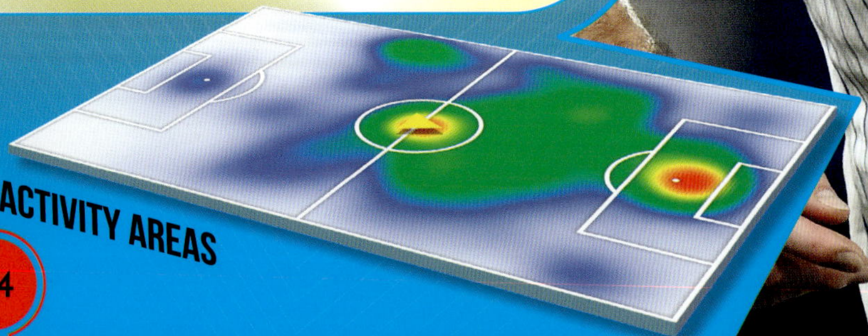

ACTIVITY AREAS

ANTOINE GRIEZMANN

A smart and hard-working forward, Griezmann can play up front, out wide, or just behind the striker. He links attacks with smart passes, makes dangerous runs, and helps teammates shine. In 2026, Atlético Madrid's all-time top scorer signed for Orlando City.

NATIONALITY
France

CURRENT CLUB
Orlando City

DATE OF BIRTH	MAR 21, 1991
POSITION	STRIKER
HEIGHT	5 FT, 9 IN
PRO DEBUT	2009
PREFERRED FOOT	LEFT

GOALS	256
PENALTIES SCORED	16
ASSISTS	109
GOALS RIGHT	36
SHOTS	1,578
HEADED GOALS	31
HAT-TRICKS	5
GOALS LEFT	189
APPEARANCES	696
SHOT CONVERSION	16.2%
MINUTES PER GOAL	202

MAJOR CLUB HONORS

- UEFA Champions League: runner-up 2016 (Atlético Madrid)
- UEFA Europa League 2018 (Atlético Madrid)
- UEFA Super Cup 2018 (Atlético Madrid)
- Copa del Rey 2021 (Barcelona)

INTERNATIONAL HONORS

- FIFA World Cup: 2018, runner-up 2022
- UEFA European Championship: runner-up 2016
- UEFA Nations League: 2021

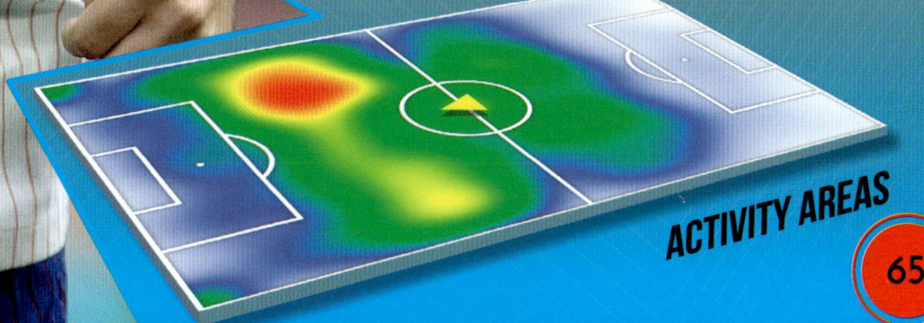

ACTIVITY AREAS

NATIONALITY
Norway

CURRENT CLUB
Manchester City

ERLING HAALAND

A goal machine for Manchester City and Norway, Haaland is one of soccer's most feared strikers. Tall, fast, and powerful, he can finish with either foot, win headers, and time his runs perfectly. In 2025–26, he won his third Premier League Golden Boot.

DATE OF BIRTH	JUL 21, 2000
POSITION	STRIKER
HEIGHT	6 FT, 5 IN
PRO DEBUT	2015
PREFERRED FOOT	LEFT

GOALS 234
PENALTIES SCORED 38
ASSISTS 45
GOALS RIGHT 34
SHOTS 918
HEADED GOALS 29
HAT-TRICKS 13
GOALS LEFT 170
APPEARANCES 263
SHOT CONVERSION 25.5%
MINUTES PER GOAL 91

MAJOR CLUB HONORS

⚽ Premier League: 2023, 2024 ⚽ UEFA Champions League: 2023 ⚽ DFB-Pokal: 2021 (Borussia Dortmund) ⚽ Austrian Bundesliga: 2019, 2020 (Red Bull Salzburg) ⚽ FA Cup: 2023, runner-up 2024, runner-up 2025, 2026 ⚽ Austrian Cup: 2019 (Red Bull Salzburg)

INTERNATIONAL HONORS

⚽ None to date

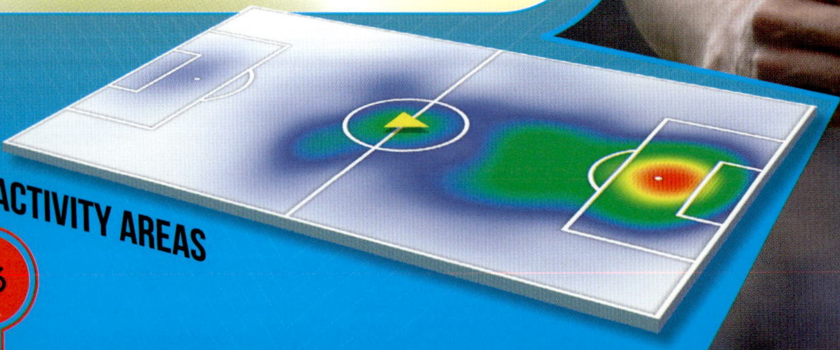

ACTIVITY AREAS

ALEXANDER ISAK

A smooth and skillful striker, Isak can score with either foot, link play, and glide past defenders. After starring for Newcastle, he made a British-record move to Liverpool in 2025. Injuries disrupted his first season, but his speed, movement, and cool finishing still make him dangerous.

NATIONALITY
Sweden

CURRENT CLUB
Newcastle

DATE OF BIRTH	SEP 21, 1999
POSITION	STRIKER
HEIGHT	6 FT, 4 IN
PRO DEBUT	2016
PREFERRED FOOT	RIGHT

- GOALS: 107
- PENALTIES SCORED: 17
- ASSISTS: 21
- GOALS RIGHT: 76
- SHOTS: 553
- HEADED GOALS: 10
- HAT-TRICKS: 3
- GOALS LEFT: 20
- APPEARANCES: 256
- SHOT CONVERSION: 19.4%
- MINUTES PER GOAL: 154

MAJOR CLUB HONORS

⚽ Football League Cup: 2025 (Newcastle United ⚽ Copa del Rey 2020 (Real Sociedad) ⚽ DFB-Pokal: 2017 (Borussia Dortmund)

INTERNATIONAL HONORS

⚽ None to date

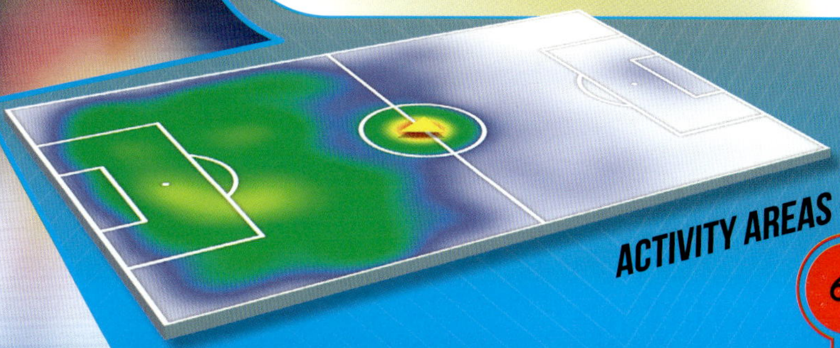

ACTIVITY AREAS

NATIONALITY
Serbia

CURRENT CLUB
AEK Athens

LUKA JOVIĆ

A sharp Serbian striker, Jović comes alive in the penalty box. He finds space quickly, finishes with smart touches, and can score with either foot or his head. After leaving AC Milan, he joined AEK Athens and rediscovered his scoring touch in Greece's top division.

DATE OF BIRTH	DEC 23, 1997
POSITION	STRIKER
HEIGHT	5 FT, 11 IN
PRO DEBUT	2014
PREFERRED FOOT	RIGHT

GOALS 83
PENALTIES SCORED 7
ASSISTS 16
GOALS RIGHT 42
SHOTS 484
HEADED GOALS 18
HAT-TRICKS 3
GOALS LEFT 23
APPEARANCES 259
SHOT CONVERSION 17.2%
MINUTES PER GOAL 156

MAJOR CLUB HONORS

⚽ La Liga: 2020, 2022 (Real Madrid) ⚽ UEFA Champions League: 2022 (Real Madrid) ⚽ UEFA Conference League: runner-up 2023 (Fiorentina) ⚽ DFB-Pokal: 2018 (Eintracht Frankfurt)

INTERNATIONAL HONORS

⚽ None to date

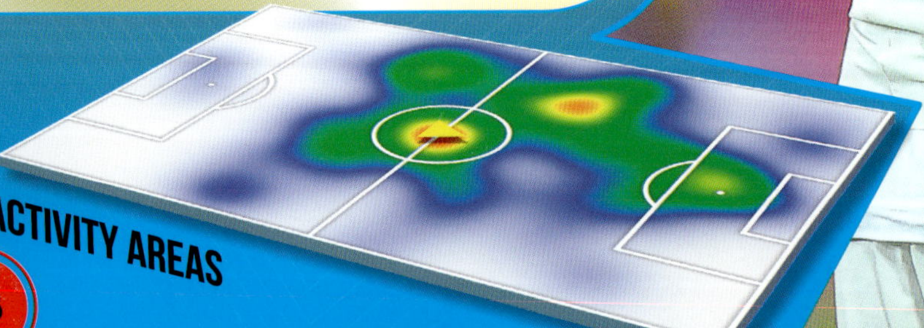

ACTIVITY AREAS

HARRY KANE

A complete striker for Bayern Munich and England, Kane can score and create goals. Powerful in the air and brilliant with both feet, he finishes coolly, links play, and picks out team-mates with smart passes. In 2025–26, he won the European Golden Shoe.

NATIONALITY
England

CURRENT CLUB
Bayern Munich

DATE OF BIRTH	JUL 28, 1993
POSITION	STRIKER
HEIGHT	6 FT, 2 IN
PRO DEBUT	2009
PREFERRED FOOT	RIGHT

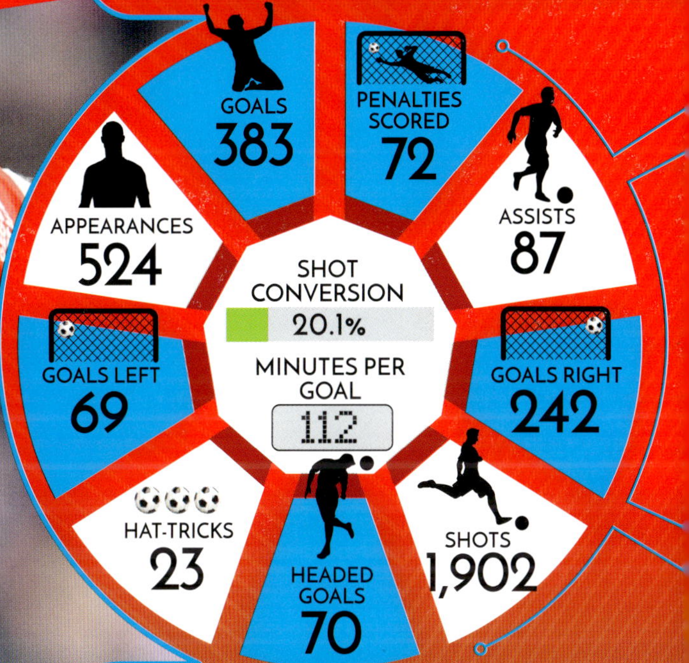

MAJOR CLUB HONORS

⚽ Bundesliga: 2025, 2026 ⚽ DFB-Pokal: 2026 ⚽ UEFA Champions League: runner-up 2019 (Tottenham Hotspur)

INTERNATIONAL HONORS

⚽ UEFA European Championship: runner-up 2020 (2021), runner-up 2024 ⚽ UEFA Nations League: third place 2019

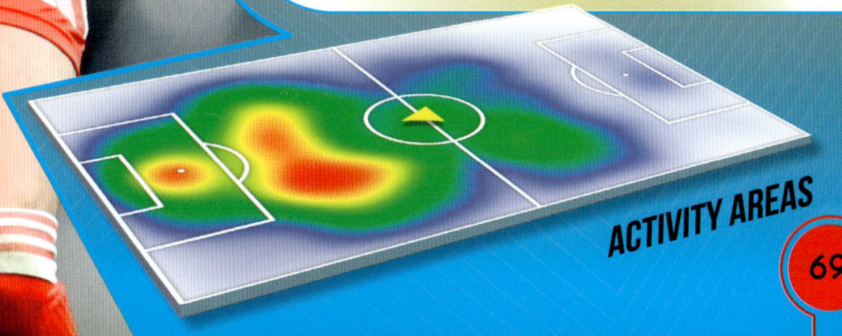

ACTIVITY AREAS

NATIONALITY
Poland

CURRENT CLUB
TBC

ROBERT LEWANDOWSKI

A legendary Polish striker, Lewandowski will go down in history as one of soccer's great finishers. Smart, powerful, and calm in front of goal, he can score with either foot or his head. After four goal-filled seasons at Barcelona, he was ready for one last big challenge.

DATE OF BIRTH	AUG 21, 1988
POSITION	STRIKER
HEIGHT	6 FT, 1 IN
PRO DEBUT	2005
PREFERRED FOOT	RIGHT

GOALS	507
PENALTIES SCORED	68
ASSISTS	96
GOALS RIGHT	331
SHOTS	2,459
HEADED GOALS	83
HAT-TRICKS	25
GOALS LEFT	88
APPEARANCES	679
SHOT CONVERSION	20.6%
MINUTES PER GOAL	106

MAJOR CLUB HONORS

⚽ La Liga: 2023, 2025, 2026 (all Barcelona) ⚽ Bundesliga: 2011, 2012 (all B. Dortmund), 2015, '16, '17, '18, '19, '20, '21, '22 (all B. Munich) ⚽ UEFA Champions League: 2020 (B. Munich) ⚽ FIFA Club World Cup: 2020 (B. Munich) ⚽ Copa del Rey: 2025 (Barcelona)

INTERNATIONAL HONORS

⚽ None to date

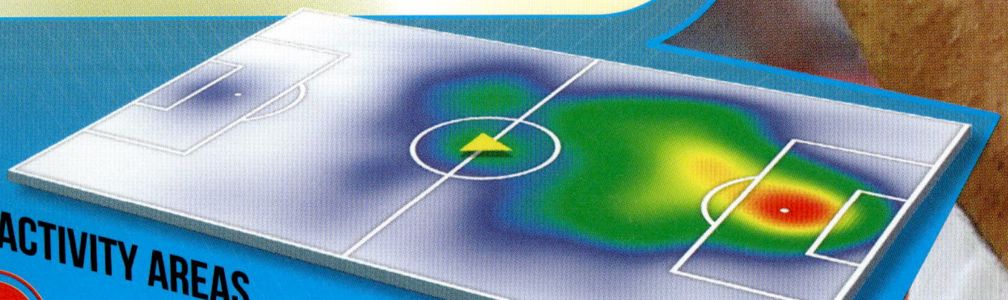

ACTIVITY AREAS

ADEMOLA LOOKMAN

A quick and skillful forward, Lookman can attack from either wing or through the middle. He uses speed, sharp touches, and smart body movement to unsettle defenders before crossing, passing, or shooting himself. After starring for Atalanta, he joined Atlético Madrid in 2026.

NATIONALITY
Nigeria

CURRENT CLUB
Atlético Madrid

DATE OF BIRTH	OCT 20, 1997
POSITION	WINGER
HEIGHT	5 FT, 9 IN
PRO DEBUT	2015
PREFERRED FOOT	BOTH

GOALS	76
PENALTIES SCORED	5
ASSISTS	37
GOALS RIGHT	51
SHOTS	502
HEADED GOALS	6
HAT-TRICKS	1
GOALS LEFT	19
APPEARANCES	285
SHOT CONVERSION	15.1%
MINUTES PER GOAL	218

MAJOR CLUB HONORS
⚽ Copa del Rey: runner-up 2026 ⚽ UEFA Europe League: 2024 (Atalanta)

INTERNATIONAL HONORS
⚽ Africa Cup of Nations: runner-up 2023, third place 2025 ⚽ FIFA U-20 World Cup: 2017 (England)

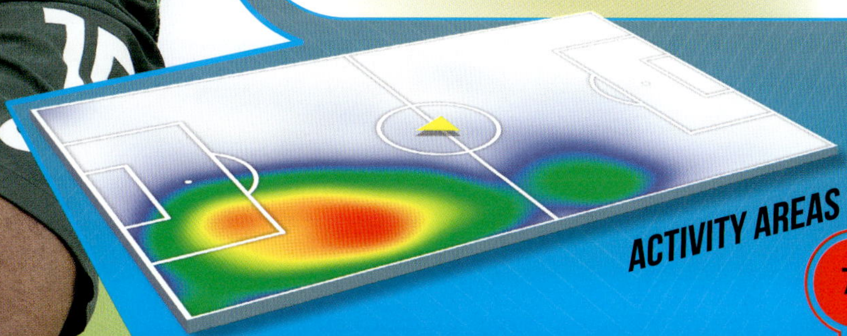

ACTIVITY AREAS

NATIONALITY
Belgium

CURRENT CLUB
Napoli

ROMELU LUKAKU

A powerful Belgian striker, Lukaku is a handful for any defense. He uses his strength to hold off defenders, bring teammates into play, and attack crosses in the box. Belgium's record goal-scorer, he remains a major threat when fully fit.

DATE OF BIRTH	MAY 13, 1993
POSITION	STRIKER
HEIGHT	6 FT, 3 IN
PRO DEBUT	2009
PREFERRED FOOT	LEFT

GOALS	252
PENALTIES SCORED	29
ASSISTS	78
GOALS RIGHT	59
SHOTS	1,301
HEADED GOALS	44
HAT-TRICKS	4
GOALS LEFT	145
APPEARANCES	538
SHOT CONVERSION	19.4%
MINUTES PER GOAL	158

MAJOR CLUB HONORS

- Serie A: 2021 (Inter Milan), 2025
- UEFA Champions League: runner-up 2023 (Inter Milan)
- Coppa Italia: 2023 (Inter Milan)
- FIFA Club World Cup: 2021 (Chelsea)
- UEFA Europa League: runner-up 2020 (Chelsea)

INTERNATIONAL HONORS

- FIFA World Cup: third place 2018

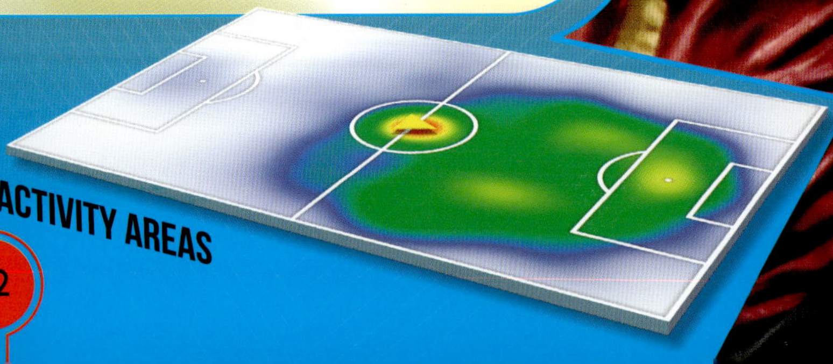

ACTIVITY AREAS

KYLIAN MBAPPÉ

A superstar striker for Real Madrid and France, Mbappé is one of soccer's most dangerous attackers. His explosive pace, sharp finishing, and smart passes make him almost impossible to stop. In 2025–26, he led the Champions League scoring charts again.

NATIONALITY
France

CURRENT CLUB
Real Madrid

DATE OF BIRTH	DEC 20, 1998
POSITION	STRIKER
HEIGHT	5 FT, 10 IN
PRO DEBUT	2015
PREFERRED FOOT	RIGHT

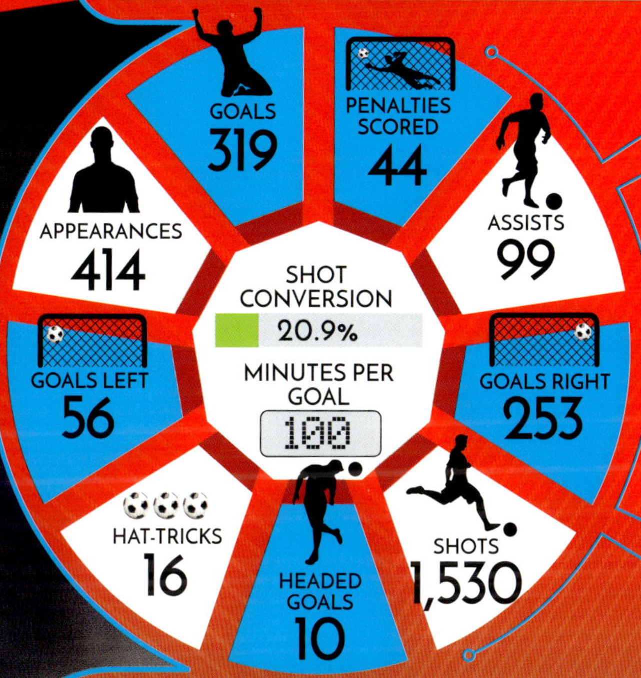

MAJOR CLUB HONORS

⚽ Ligue 1: 2017 (Monaco), 2018, 2019, 2020, 2022, 2023, 2024 (all PSG) ⚽ Supercopa de España: 2026 ⚽ UEFA Champions League: runner-up 2020 (PSG) ⚽ Coupe de France: 2018, 2020, 2021, 2024 (all PSG) ⚽ FIFA Intercontinental Cup: 2024

INTERNATIONAL HONORS

⚽ FIFA World Cup: 2018, runner-up 2022
⚽ UEFA Nations League: 2021

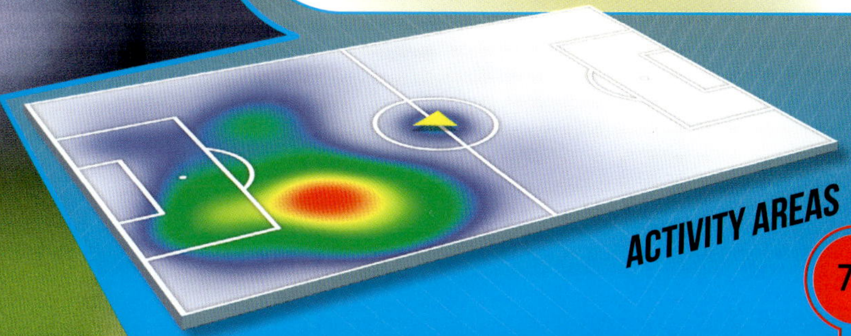

NATIONALITY
Argentina

CURRENT CLUB
Inter Miami (USA)

LIONEL MESSI

A World Cup winner and eight-time Ballon d'Or champion, Messi remains one of soccer's greatest ever players. Now leading Argentina into a sixth World Cup, he still uses magical close control, smart passes and cool finishing to create danger for club and country.

DATE OF BIRTH	JUN 24, 1987
POSITION	FORWARD
HEIGHT	5 FT, 7 IN
PRO DEBUT	2003
PREFERRED FOOT	LEFT

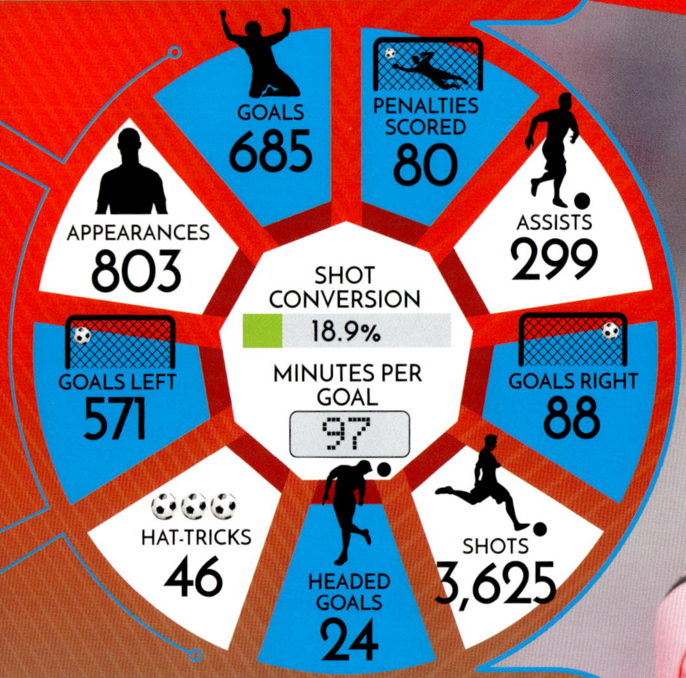

MAJOR CLUB HONORS

⚽ Ligue 1: 2022, 2023 (PSG) ⚽ La Liga: 2005, '06, '09, '10 '11, '13, '15, '16, '18, '19 (all Barça) ⚽ UEFA Champions League: 2006, '09, '11, '15 (all Barça) ⚽ UEFA Super Cup: 2009, '11, '15 (all Barça) ⚽ FIFA Club World Cup: 2009, '11, '15 (all Barça) ⚽ MLS Leagues Cup: 2023 ⚽ MLS Cup: 2025

INTERNATIONAL HONORS

- FIFA World Cup: 2022, runner-up 2014
- Olympic Games: gold medal 2008
- Copa América: 2021, 2024, runner-up* 2007*, 2015*, 2016*

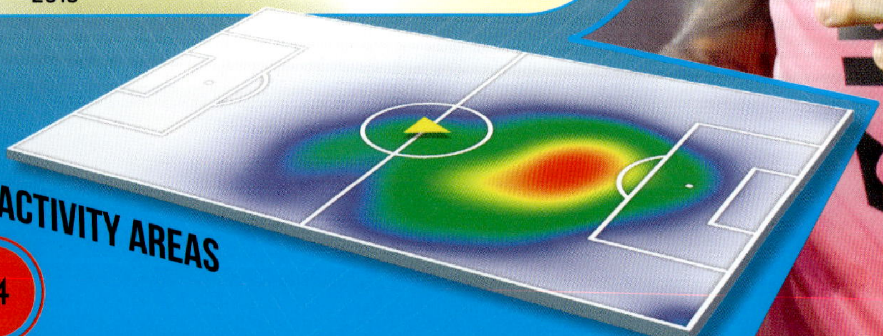

ACTIVITY AREAS

ÁLVARO MORATA

A smart Spanish striker, Morata uses strength, movement, and experience to trouble defenders. Strong in the air and calm with the ball, he can lead the line or link attacks. After captaining Spain to EURO 2024 glory, he continued his career in Serie A with Como.

NATIONALITY
Spain

CURRENT CLUB
AC Milan (on loan at Como)

DATE OF BIRTH	OCT 23, 1992
POSITION	STRIKER
HEIGHT	6 FT, 3 IN
PRO DEBUT	2010
PREFERRED FOOT	RIGHT

- GOALS 164
- PENALTIES SCORED 7
- ASSISTS 58
- GOALS RIGHT 83
- SHOTS 936
- HEADED GOALS 41
- HAT-TRICKS 3
- GOALS LEFT 40
- APPEARANCES 506
- SHOT CONVERSION 17.5%
- MINUTES PER GOAL 168

MAJOR CLUB HONORS

La Liga: 2012, 2017 (R. Madrid) Serie A: 2015, 2016 (all Juventus) UEFA Champions League: 2014, '17 (R. Madrid), runner-up 2015 (Juventus) UEFA Europa League: 2019 (Chelsea) UEFA Super Cup: 2016 (R. Madrid) FIFA Club World Cup: 2016 (R. Madrid)

INTERNATIONAL HONORS

- UEFA European Championship: 2024
- UEFA Nations League: 2023, runner-up 2025
- UEFA European U-21 Championship: 2013

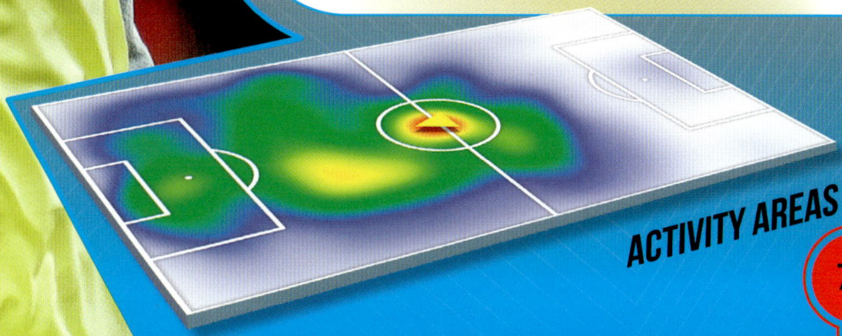

ACTIVITY AREAS

NATIONALITY
Brazil

CURRENT CLUB
Santos (Brazil)

NEYMAR

Back at Santos, where his career began, Neymar remains one of Brazil's most gifted attackers. Brazil's all-time leading scorer, he can still unlock defenses with close control, tricks, and smart passes. In 2026, he raced to recover from injury before the World Cup.

DATE OF BIRTH	FEB 5, 1992
POSITION	FORWARD
HEIGHT	5 FT, 9 IN
PRO DEBUT	2009
PREFERRED FOOT	RIGHT

GOALS 233
PENALTIES SCORED 41
ASSISTS 124
GOALS RIGHT 156
SHOTS 1,174
HEADED GOALS 8
HAT-TRICKS 11
GOALS LEFT 55
APPEARANCES 396
SHOT CONVERSION 19.9%
MINUTES PER GOAL 138

MAJOR CLUB HONORS

⚽ La Liga: 2015, '16, '17 (all Barça) ⚽ Ligue 1: 2018, '19 '20, 2022, 2023 (all PSG) ⚽ UEFA Champions League: 2016 (Barça), runner-up 2020 (PSG) ⚽ FIFA Club World Cup: 2016 (Barça) ⚽ Copa del Rey: 2015, '16, '17 (all Barça) ⚽ Coupe de France: 2018, '20, '21 (all PSG)

INTERNATIONAL HONORS

- ⚽ Copa América: runner-up 2021
- ⚽ FIFA Confederations Cup: 2013
- ⚽ Olympic Games: silver medal 2012, gold medal 2016

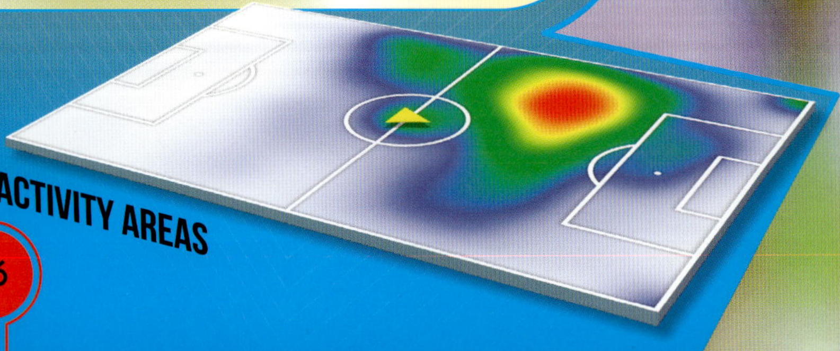

ACTIVITY AREAS

JOÃO PEDRO

A smart and skillful forward, João Pedro can play behind the striker or lead the line himself. He has a sharp first touch, dribbles past defenders, and fires powerful shots. After joining Chelsea in 2025, he made an instant impact in the summer at the Club World Cup.

NATIONALITY
Brazil

CURRENT CLUB
Chelsea

20

DATE OF BIRTH	SEP 26, 2001
POSITION	SECOND STRIKER
HEIGHT	5 FT, 9 IN
PRO DEBUT	2009
PREFERRED FOOT	RIGHT

- GOALS 53
- PENALTIES SCORED 13
- ASSISTS 16
- GOALS RIGHT 36
- SHOTS 336
- HEADED GOALS 8
- HAT-TRICKS 1
- GOALS LEFT 9
- APPEARANCES 166
- SHOT CONVERSION 15.8%
- MINUTES PER GOAL 211

NEW ENTRY!

MAJOR CLUB HONORS
- FIFA World Club Cup: 2025
- FA Cup: runner-up 2026

INTERNATIONAL HONORS
- None to date

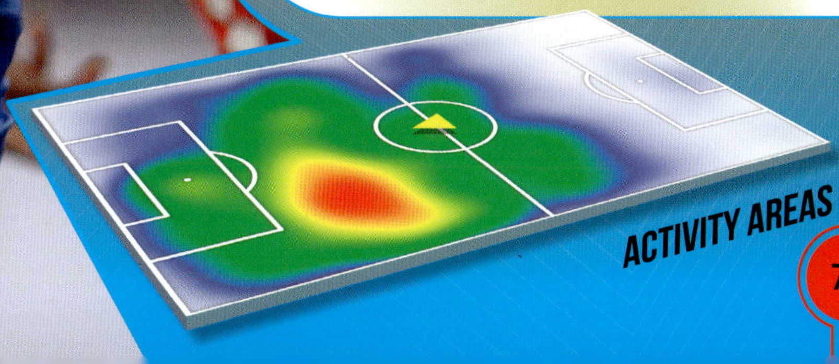

ACTIVITY AREAS

NATIONALITY
Portugal

CURRENT CLUB
Al-Nassr (S. Arabia)

CRISTIANO RONALDO

A legendary Portuguese striker, Ronaldo remains one of soccer's greatest goal-scorers. Now leading Portugal into a sixth World Cup, he still brings power, heading ability, and ruthless finishing in the box. With more than 900 career goals, he is a true soccer icon.

DATE OF BIRTH	FEB 2, 1985
POSITION	FORWARD
HEIGHT	6 FT, 2 IN
PRO DEBUT	2002
PREFERRED FOOT	RIGHT

GOALS 732
PENALTIES SCORED 145
ASSISTS 191
GOALS RIGHT 490
SHOTS 4,904
HEADED GOALS 113
HAT-TRICKS 53
GOALS LEFT 126
APPEARANCES 850
SHOT CONVERSION 14.9%
MINUTES PER GOAL 99

MAJOR CLUB HONORS

UEFA Champions League: 2008 (Man. U), 2014, '16, '17, '18 (R. Madrid) FIFA Club World Cup: 2008 (Man. U), 2014, '16, '17 (R. Madrid) UEFA Super Cup: 2014, '17 (R. Madrid) Serie A: 2019, '20 (Juventus) Premier League: 2007, '08, '09 (Man. U) La Liga: 2012, '17 (R. Madrid) Saudi Pro League: 2026

INTERNATIONAL HONORS

- UEFA European Championship: 2016
- UEFA Nations League: 2019, 2025

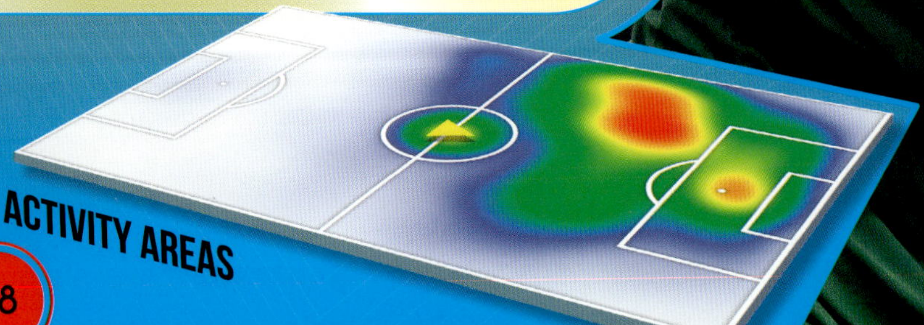

ACTIVITY AREAS

MOHAMED SALAH

A brilliant left-footed attacker, Salah is one of Liverpool and Egypt's greatest ever players. He cuts in from the right wing, using pace, sharp movement, and cool finishing to punish defenses. In 2026, he left Liverpool as a record-breaking Premier League legend.

NATIONALITY
Egypt

CURRENT CLUB
TBC

DATE OF BIRTH	JUN 15, 1992
POSITION	WINGER
HEIGHT	5 FT, 9 IN
PRO DEBUT	2010
PREFERRED FOOT	LEFT

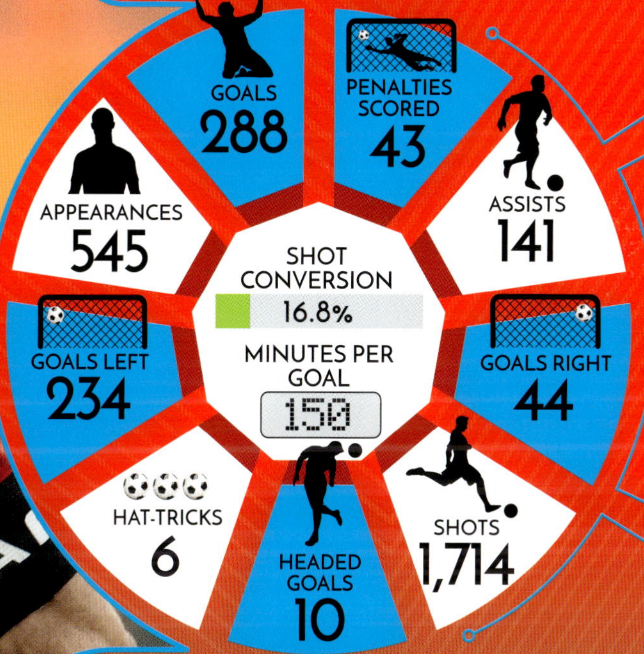

MAJOR CLUB HONORS

⚽ Premier League: 2020, 2025 (all Liverpool) ⚽ UEFA Champions League: 2019, runner-up 2018, runner-up 2022 (all Liverpool) ⚽ UEFA Super Cup: 2019 (Liverpool) ⚽ FIFA Club World Cup: 2019 (Liverpool) ⚽ FA Cup: 2022 (Liverpool)

INTERNATIONAL HONORS

⚽ CAF Africa Cup of Nations: runner-up 2017, runner-up 2021

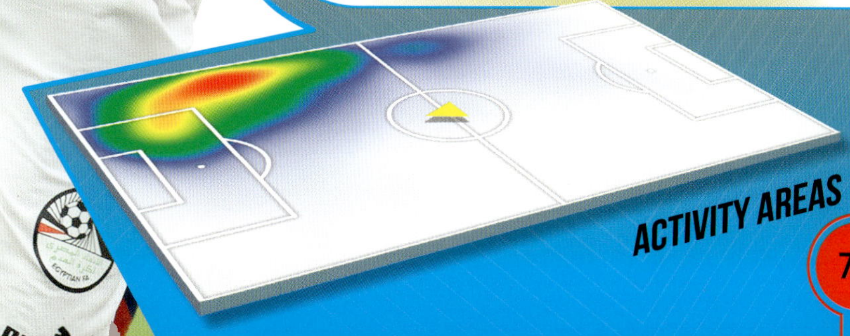

ACTIVITY AREAS

NATIONALITY
South Korea

CURRENT CLUB
Los Angeles FC

SON HEUNG-MIN

A two-footed South Korean superstar, Son can play wide, centrally, or just behind the striker. He times his runs perfectly, finishes calmly, and shoots powerfully with either foot. After becoming a Tottenham legend, he began a new chapter in Major League Soccer with LAFC.

DATE OF BIRTH	JUL 8, 1992
POSITION	WINGER
HEIGHT	6 FT
PRO DEBUT	2010
PREFERRED FOOT	BOTH

GOALS	209
PENALTIES SCORED	5
ASSISTS	93
GOALS RIGHT	118
SHOTS	1,244
HEADED GOALS	10
HAT-TRICKS	7
GOALS LEFT	81
APPEARANCES	565
SHOT CONVERSION	16.8%
MINUTES PER GOAL	192

MAJOR CLUB HONORS

- UEFA Champions League: runner-up 2019 (Tottenham)
- UEFA Europa League: 2025 (Tottenham)

INTERNATIONAL HONORS

- AFC Asian Cup: runner-up 2015

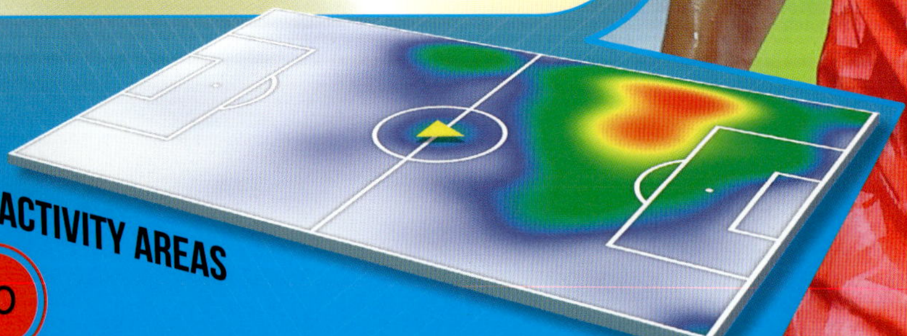

ACTIVITY AREAS

VINÍCIUS JÚNIOR

A fearless Brazilian winger, Vinícius Júnior attacks from the left with electric pace and dazzling skill. He loves running at right-backs, cutting inside, and creating danger with crosses, passes, or shots. In 2026, he aimed to bring his Real Madrid magic to Brazil's World Cup campaign.

NATIONALITY
Brazil

CURRENT CLUB
Real Madrid

DATE OF BIRTH	JUL 12, 2000
POSITION	WINGER
HEIGHT	5 FT, 9 IN
PRO DEBUT	2017
PREFERRED FOOT	RIGHT

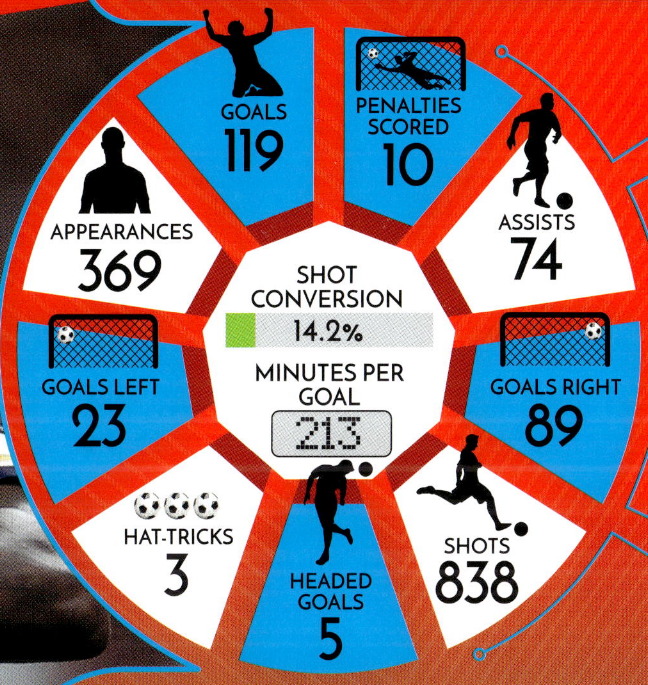

MAJOR CLUB HONORS

⚽ La Liga: 2020, 2022, 2024 ⚽ UEFA Champions League: 2022, 2024 ⚽ FIFA Club World Cup: 2018, 2022 ⚽ UEFA Super Cup: 2022 ⚽ Copa del Rey: 2023 ⚽ FIFA Intercontinental Cup: 2024

INTERNATIONAL HONORS

⚽ Copa América: runner-up 2021

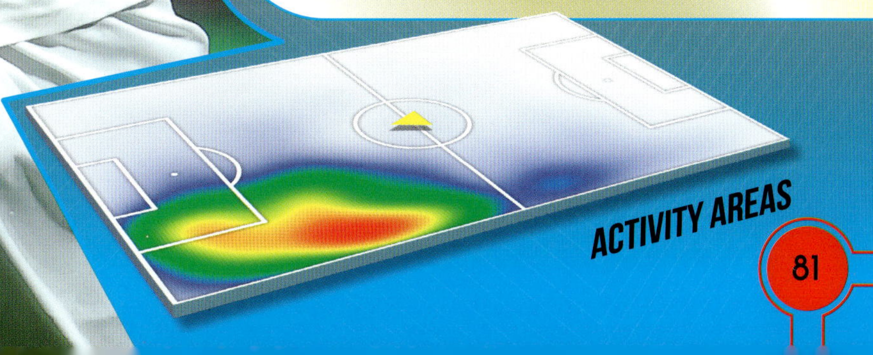

ACTIVITY AREAS

10

NATIONALITY
Spain

CURRENT CLUB
Athletic Club (Bilbao)

NICO WILLIAMS

A fast and fearless winger for Athletic Bilbao and Spain, Williams loves attacking defenders from the left. He uses explosive pace, quick feet, and sharp crosses to create chances. After starring in Spain's EURO 2024 win, he committed his future to Athletic until 2035.

DATE OF BIRTH	JUL 12, 2002
POSITION	LEFT-WINGER
HEIGHT	5 FT, 11 IN
PRO DEBUT	2020
PREFERRED FOOT	RIGHT

GOALS 27

PENALTIES SCORED 1

ASSISTS 25

APPEARANCES 173

SHOT CONVERSION 9.5%

MINUTES PER GOAL 413

GOALS LEFT 10

GOALS RIGHT 15

HAT-TRICKS 0

HEADED GOALS 2

SHOTS 283

MAJOR CLUB HONORS
- Copa del Rey: 2024

INTERNATIONAL HONORS
- UEFA European Championship: 2024
- UEFA Nations League: runner-up 2025

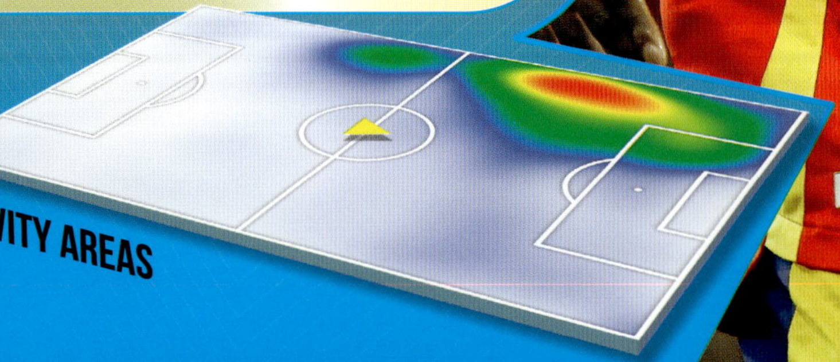

ACTIVITY AREAS

LAMINE YAMAL

A dazzling Barcelona and Spain winger, Yamal is already one of soccer's brightest stars. Left-footed and fearless, he beats defenders with quick feet, curls dangerous crosses toward goal, and creates chances from the right. In 2026, he headed to his first World Cup with Spain.

NATIONALITY
Spain

CURRENT CLUB
Barcelona

19

DATE OF BIRTH	JUL 13, 2007
POSITION	RIGHT-WINGER
HEIGHT	5 FT, 11 IN
PRO DEBUT	2023
PREFERRED FOOT	LEFT

- GOALS: 41
- PENALTIES SCORED: 6
- ASSISTS: 38
- GOALS RIGHT: 4
- SHOTS: 429
- HEADED GOALS: 0
- HAT-TRICKS: 1
- GOALS LEFT: 37
- APPEARANCES: 134
- SHOT CONVERSION: 9.6%
- MINUTES PER GOAL: 241

MAJOR CLUB HONORS

- La Liga 2023, 2025, 2026
- Copa del Rey: 2025
- Supercopa de España: 2025, 2026

INTERNATIONAL HONORS

- UEFA European Championship: 2024
- UEFA Nations League: runner-up 2024

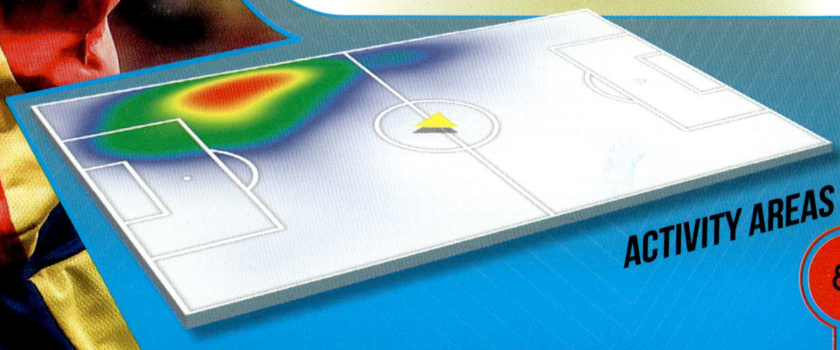

ACTIVITY AREAS

GOALKEEPERS

Goalkeepers are the last line of defense. They stand alone in front of goal, where one mistake can give the other team a huge chance to score. That makes it one of soccer's toughest jobs, demanding bravery, focus, and fast reactions. The stars in this section are all amazing shot-stoppers, but each has special skills. Their heat maps show what type of keeper they are: some stay close to goal, some race out like sweeper-keepers, and others help start attacks from the back.

WHAT DO THE STATS MEAN?

CATCHES

This is the number of times the keeper has dealt with an attack—usually a cross—by catching the ball.

CLEAN SHEETS

Any occasion on which the goalie has not let in a goal for the full duration of the game counts as a clean sheet.

GOALS CONCEDED

This is the number of goals the keeper has conceded in their career in top-division soccer.

PENALTIES FACED/SAVED

This is the number of times a goalie has faced a penalty (excludes shoot-outs) and how successful he has been at saving it.

PUNCHES

This is a measure of how often the keeper has dealt with a dangerous ball (usually a cross) by punching it clear.

SAVES

This shows how many times the goalkeeper has stopped a shot or header that was on target.

Did you know?

Goalkeepers can, in theory, score goals with their hands. If they throw a ball downfield and it goes directly into the opposition net, the goal will count but, of course, the ball would have to travel more than 300 feet, which is unlikely.

NATIONALITY
Brazil

CURRENT CLUB
Liverpool

ALISSON

A world-class Brazilian goalkeeper, Alisson has been a huge player for Liverpool since 2018. He is a superb shot-stopper, strong on crosses, and quick off his line to stop danger. With calm short passes or long kicks, he can turn defense into attack.

DATE OF BIRTH	OCT 2, 1992
POSITION	GOALKEEPER
HEIGHT	6 FT, 4 IN
PRO DEBUT	2013
PREFERRED FOOT	RIGHT

MAJOR CLUB HONORS
- Premier League: 2020, 2025
- UEFA Champions League: 2019, runner-up 2022
- FIFA Club World Cup: 2019
- FA Cup: 2022

INTERNATIONAL HONORS
- Copa América: 2019, runner-up 2021

ACTIVITY AREAS

THIBAUT COURTOIS

A giant presence in goal, Courtois uses his height and reach to make difficult saves look simple. He dominates crosses, commands his penalty area, and reacts quickly to low shots. Back to his best after injury, he helped Real Madrid stay solid in 2025–26.

NATIONALITY
Belgium

CURRENT CLUB
Real Madrid

DATE OF BIRTH	MAY 11, 1992
POSITION	GOALKEEPER
HEIGHT	6 FT, 6 IN
PRO DEBUT	2009
PREFERRED FOOT	LEFT

MAJOR CLUB HONORS
⚽ La Liga: 2014 (At. Mad.), 2020, 2022, runner-up 2023, 2024 ⚽ Prem. League: 2015, 2017 (all Chelsea) ⚽ UEFA Champ. League: 2022, 2024 ⚽ UEFA Europa League: 2012 (At. Mad.) ⚽ FIFA Club World Cup: 2018 ⚽ UEFA Super Cup: 2012 (At. Mad.) 2022 ⚽ Copa del Rey: 2013 (At Mad), 2023

INTERNATIONAL HONORS
⚽ FIFA World Cup: third place 2018

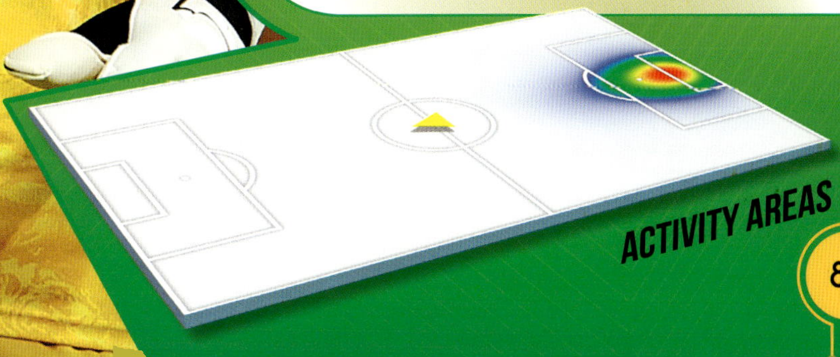

ACTIVITY AREAS

NATIONALITY
Italy

CURRENT CLUB
Manchester City

GIANLUIGI DONNARUMMA

A giant Italian goalkeeper, Donnarumma became a first-team regular at just 16. Now at Manchester City, he brings size, bravery, and huge experience to the goal. He commands his area, saves bravely at forwards' feet, and uses quick reactions to stop powerful shots.

DATE OF BIRTH	FEB 25, 1999
POSITION	GOALKEEPER
HEIGHT	6 FT, 5 IN
PRO DEBUT	2015
PREFERRED FOOT	RIGHT

MAJOR CLUB HONORS

⚽ Ligue 1: 2022, 2023, 2024, 2025 (all PSG) ⚽ UEFA Champions League: 2025 (PSG) ⚽ FA Cup: 2026 ⚽ EFL Cup: 2026 ⚽ Coupe de France: 2024, 2025 ⚽ Supercoppa Italiana: 2016 (AC Milan)

INTERNATIONAL HONORS

⚽ UEFA European Championship: 2020 (2021)
⚽ UEFA Nations League: third place 2021, third place 2023

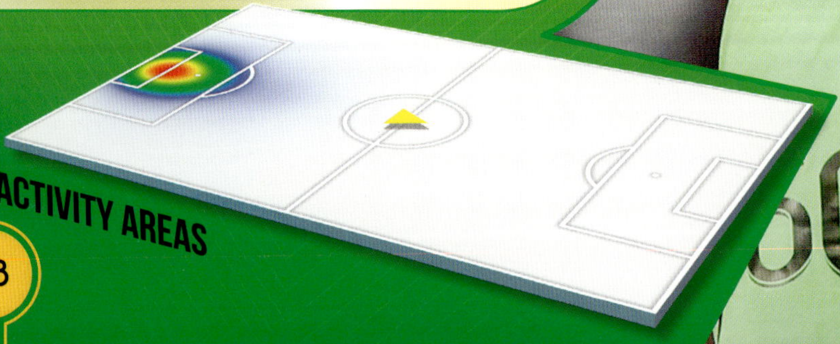

ACTIVITY AREAS

JOAN GARCIA

A rising Spanish goalkeeper, Garcia has the calm and reflexes needed at the very top. He times his runs off the line, saves bravely, and stays composed under pressure. After joining Barcelona from Espanyol, he won La Liga's Zamora Trophy in 2025–26.

NATIONALITY
Spain

CURRENT CLUB
Barcelona

DATE OF BIRTH	MAY 4, 2001
POSITION	GOALKEEPER
HEIGHT	6 FT, 4 IN
PRO DEBUT	2021
PREFERRED FOOT	RIGHT

MAJOR CLUB HONORS
- La Liga 2026
- Supercopa de España: 2026

INTERNATIONAL HONORS
- Summer Olympic Games: Gold 2024

ACTIVITY AREAS

NATIONALITY
Hungary

CURRENT CLUB
RB Leipzig

PÉTER GULÁCSI

A calm and experienced goalkeeper, Gulácsi uses smart positioning to make difficult saves look simple. He studies attackers carefully, reacts quickly, and gets his body in the right place. After extending his RB Leipzig stay to 2027, he remained a trusted figure at the club.

DATE OF BIRTH	MAY 6, 1990
POSITION	GOALKEEPER
HEIGHT	6 FT, 3 IN
PRO DEBUT	2008
PREFERRED FOOT	RIGHT

MAJOR CLUB HONORS

- Austrian Bundesliga: 2014, 2015 (Red Bull Salzburg)
- Austrian Cup: 2014, 2015 (Red Bull Salzburg)
- DFB-Pokal: runner-up 2019, runner-up 2021*, 2022, 2023

INTERNATIONAL HONORS

- FIFA U-20 World Cup: third place 2009

ACTIVITY AREAS

LUKAS HRADECKY

A late-blooming Finnish goalkeeper, Hradecký reached new heights in his thirties. He captained Bayer Leverkusen to their historic Bundesliga title, then joined Monaco in 2025. Confident on crosses and sharp with his positioning, he organizes defenders and makes hard saves look simple.

NATIONALITY
Finland

CURRENT CLUB
Monaco

DATE OF BIRTH	NOV 24, 1989
POSITION	GOALKEEPER
HEIGHT	6 FT, 4 IN
PRO DEBUT	2008
PREFERRED FOOT	RIGHT

GOALS CONCEDED 499

APPEARANCES 389

PENALTIES SAVED 6

SAVES 1,083

CLEAN SHEETS 106

PENALTIES FACED 45

CATCHES 96

PUNCHES 135

MAJOR CLUB HONORS

⚽ Bundesliga: 2024 (Bayer Leverkusen) ⚽ DFB Pokal: 2018 (Eintracht Frankfurt), 2024 (Bayer Leverkusen) ⚽ UEFA Europa League: runner-up 2024 (Bayer Leverkusen)

INTERNATIONAL HONORS

⚽ Baltic Cup: Runner-up 2012

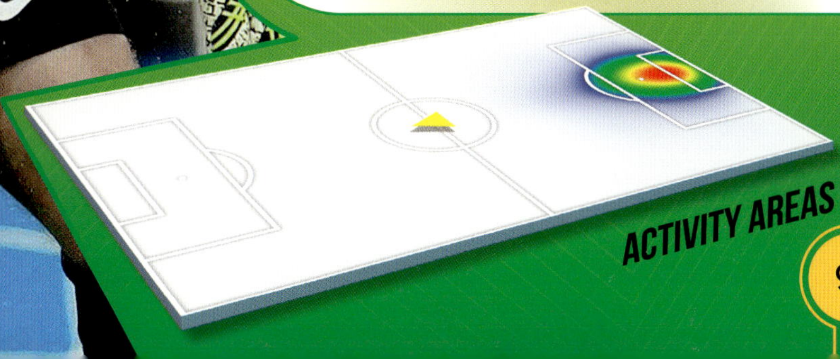

ACTIVITY AREAS

NATIONALITY
France

CURRENT CLUB
AC Milan

MIKE MAIGNAN

A powerful French goalkeeper, Maignan is known for explosive close-range saves and big leadership. He commands his box, talks constantly to defenders, and uses sharp distribution to start attacks. AC Milan's captain, he remained one of Europe's most respected keepers in 2025–26.

DATE OF BIRTH	JUL 3, 1995
POSITION	GOALKEEPER
HEIGHT	6 FT, 3 IN
PRO DEBUT	2012
PREFERRED FOOT	RIGHT

GOALS CONCEDED 365
APPEARANCES 352
PENALTIES SAVED 14
SAVES 939
CLEAN SHEETS 123
PENALTIES FACED 58
CATCHES 43
PUNCHES 94

MAJOR CLUB HONORS

- Serie A: 2022
- Supercoppa Italiana: 2024
- Ligue 1: 2021 (Lille)

INTERNATIONAL HONORS

- UEFA Nations League 2021: third place 2025

ACTIVITY AREAS

EMILIANO MARTÍNEZ

A brilliant Argentine goalkeeper, Martínez is famous for huge saves in big moments. Athletic and brave, he can spring across goal, narrow shooting angles, and unsettle penalty-takers. In 2026, Aston Villa's World Cup winner was picked to help Argentina defend their title.

NATIONALITY
Argentina

CURRENT CLUB
Aston Villa

DATE OF BIRTH	SEP 2, 1992
POSITION	GOALKEEPER
HEIGHT	6 FT, 5 IN
PRO DEBUT	2012
PREFERRED FOOT	RIGHT

MAJOR CLUB HONORS

- UEFA Europa League: 2026
- FA Cup: 2020 (Arsenal)

INTERNATIONAL HONORS

- Copa América: 2021, 2024
- FIFA World Cup: 2022
- CONMEBOL-UEFA Cup of Champions: 2022

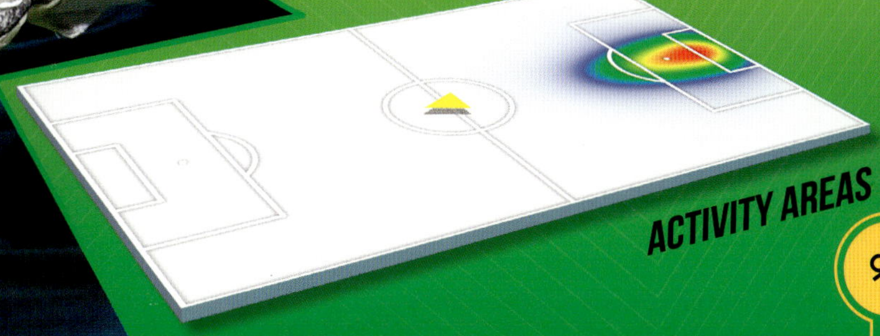

ACTIVITY AREAS

NATIONALITY
Germany

CURRENT CLUB
Bayern Munich (on loan to VfB Stuttgart)

ALEXANDER NÜBEL

A tall and athletic goalkeeper, Nübel sharpened his skills during loan spells at Monaco and Stuttgart. He uses his long reach and sharp reflexes to stop shots, win one-on-ones, and claim crosses. After three strong years at Stuttgart, his next move remained uncertain.

DATE OF BIRTH	SEP 30, 1996
POSITION	GOALKEEPER
HEIGHT	6 FT, 4 IN
PRO DEBUT	2014
PREFERRED FOOT	RIGHT

- GOALS CONCEDED 354
- APPEARANCES 258
- PENALTIES SAVED 3
- SAVES 744
- CLEAN SHEETS 66
- PENALTIES FACED 40
- CATCHES 45
- PUNCHES 61

MAJOR CLUB HONORS
⚽ Bundesliga: 2021 (Bayern Munich) ⚽ DFB-Pokal: 2025 ⚽ UEFA Super Cup: 2020 (Bayern Munich) ⚽ FIFA Club World Cup: 2020 (Bayern Munich)

INTERNATIONAL HONORS
⚽ None to date

ACTIVITY AREAS

NEW ENTRY!

MANUEL NEUER

A Bayern Munich legend, Neuer changed how goalkeepers play. The original sweeper-keeper, he races out to stop danger, commands his penalty area, and starts attacks with smart passes. Still playing at 40, he extended his Bayern contract in 2026 for one more season.

NATIONALITY
Germany

CURRENT CLUB
Bayern Munich

DATE OF BIRTH	MAR 27, 1986
POSITION	GOALKEEPER
HEIGHT	6 FT, 4 IN
PRO DEBUT	2004
PREFERRED FOOT	RIGHT

MAJOR CLUB HONORS

⚽ Bundesliga: 2013, 2014, 2015, 2016, 2017, 2018, 2019, 2020, 2021, 2022, 2023, 2025, 2026 ⚽ UEFA Champions League: 2013, 2020 ⚽ UEFA Super Cup: 2013, 2020 ⚽ FIFA Club World Cup: 2013, 2020 ⚽ DFB-Pokal 2011 (Schalke 04), 2013, 2014, 2016 2019, 2020, 2026

INTERNATIONAL HONORS

⚽ FIFA World Cup: 2014, third place 2010

ACTIVITY AREAS

NATIONALITY
Slovenia

CURRENT CLUB
Atlético Madrid

JAN OBLAK

A commanding Atlético Madrid goalkeeper, Oblak is known for sharp reflexes, calm positioning, and cool decision-making. The Slovenia captain can make huge saves, organize the back line, and stay composed in pressure moments. In 2026, he reached 100 Champions League appearances.

DATE OF BIRTH	JAN 7, 1993
POSITION	GOALKEEPER
HEIGHT	6 FT, 2 IN
PRO DEBUT	2009
PREFERRED FOOT	RIGHT

MAJOR CLUB HONORS
- La Liga: 2021
- UEFA Champions League: runner-up 2016
- UEFA Europa League: 2018
- UEFA Super Cup: 2018

INTERNATIONAL HONORS
- None to date

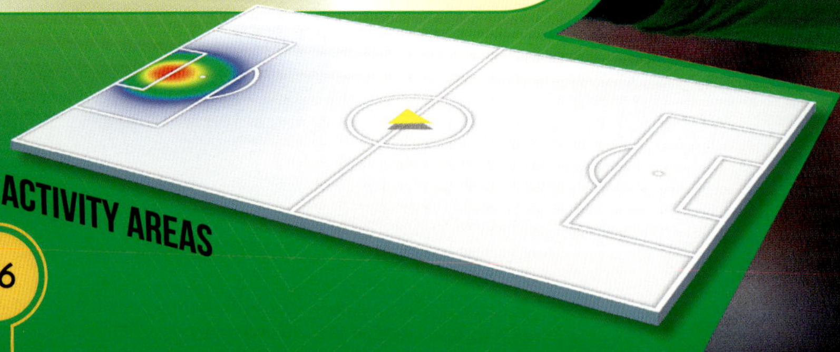

ACTIVITY AREAS

JORDAN PICKFORD

England's long-serving No. 1, Pickford is a sharp shot-stopper with big-tournament experience. He reacts quickly, spreads himself bravely in one-on-ones, and can start attacks with accurate long passes. In 2026, he was named in England's World Cup squad again.

NATIONALITY
England

CURRENT CLUB
Everton

DATE OF BIRTH	MAR 3, 1994
POSITION	GOALKEEPER
HEIGHT	6 FT, 1 IN
PRO DEBUT	2011
PREFERRED FOOT	LEFT

MAJOR CLUB HONORS
- None to date

INTERNATIONAL HONORS
- UEFA European Championship: runner-up 2020, runner-up 2024
- UEFA Natiom League: third place 2019

ACTIVITY AREAS

NATIONALITY
Italy

CURRENT CLUB
Lazio

IVAN PROVEDEL

A tall and agile Lazio goalkeeper, Provedel commands his penalty area with confidence. He catches or punches crosses, reacts sharply to close-range shots, and reads danger early. Comfortable with the ball at his feet, he can also sweep behind the defense and pass accurately from the back.

DATE OF BIRTH	MAR 17, 1994
POSITION	GOALKEEPER
HEIGHT	6 FT, 4 IN
PRO DEBUT	2013
PREFERRED FOOT	RIGHT

GOALS CONCEDED 300
APPEARANCES 218
CLEAN SHEETS 63
CATCHES 16
PUNCHES 84
PENALTIES FACED 38
PENALTIES SAVED 3
SAVES 643

MAJOR CLUB HONORS

- UEFA Europa Conference League: 2022 (Roma)
- UEFA Europa League: runner-up 2023 (Roma)

INTERNATIONAL HONORS

- UEFA European Championship: 2016
- UEFA Natiom League: 2019

ACTIVITY AREAS

NEW ENTRY!

DAVID RAYA

A brilliant Spanish goalkeeper, Raya gives Arsenal confidence from the back. He claims crosses, reacts quickly to shots, and uses smart passes to help his defenders play higher up the field. In 2025–26, he won a third straight Premier League Golden Glove after 19 clean sheets.

NATIONALITY
Spain

CURRENT CLUB
Arsenal

DATE OF BIRTH	SEP 15, 1995
POSITION	GOALKEEPER
HEIGHT	6 FT
PRO DEBUT	2014
PREFERRED FOOT	RIGHT

GOALS CONCEDED	178
APPEARANCES	205
PENALTIES SAVED	3
SAVES	509
CLEAN SHEETS	87
PENALTIES FACED	19
PUNCHES	51
CATCHES	34

MAJOR CLUB HONORS

- Premier League: 2026
- UEFA Champions League: runner-up 2026

INTERNATIONAL HONORS

- UEFA European Championship: 2024
- UEFA Nations League: 2023 runner-up 2025

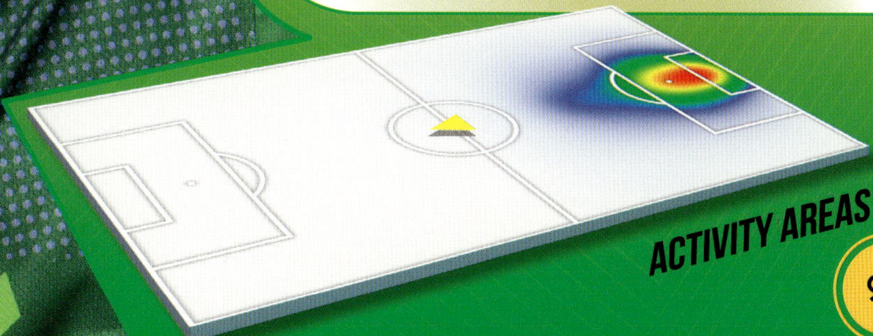

ACTIVITY AREAS

NATIONALITY
France

CURRENT CLUB
Rennes

BRICE SAMBA

Samba brings strength, voice, and presence to Rennes. He organizes defenders, claims crosses, and uses his body bravely to block shots. Excellent at saving penalties, he also distributes well, sending accurate passes downfield to help his team attack.

DATE OF BIRTH	APR 25, 1994
POSITION	GOALKEEPER
HEIGHT	6 FT, 1 IN
PRO DEBUT	2011
PREFERRED FOOT	LEFT

MAJOR CLUB HONORS

- None to date

INTERNATIONAL HONORS

- UEFA Nations League: third place 2025

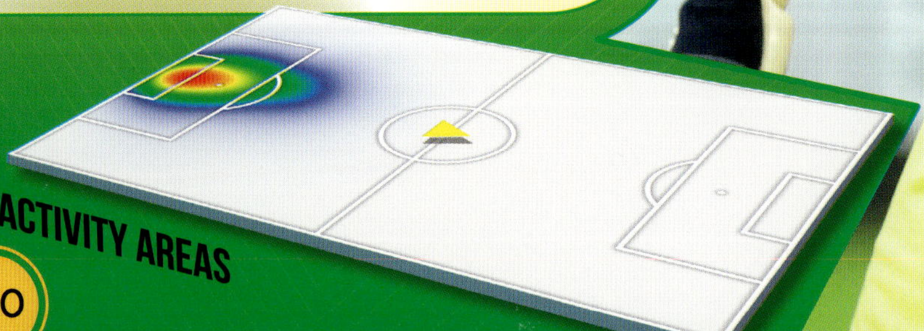

ACTIVITY AREAS

ROBERT SÁNCHEZ

Quick off his line and brave in one-on-ones, Robert Sánchez gives Chelsea a strong presence in goal. He communicates well with his defenders, helps his team play out from the back, and reacts sharply to close-range shots. In 2025, he won the Club World Cup Golden Glove.

NATIONALITY
Spain

CURRENT CLUB
Chelsea

DATE OF BIRTH	NOV 18, 1997
POSITION	GOALKEEPER
HEIGHT	6 FT, 6 IN
PRO DEBUT	2018
PREFERRED FOOT	RIGHT

MAJOR CLUB HONORS

- FIFA World Club Cup: 2025
- UEFA Conference League: 2025
- EFL Cup: runner-up: 2024

INTERNATIONAL HONORS

- UEFA Nations League: runner-up 2021

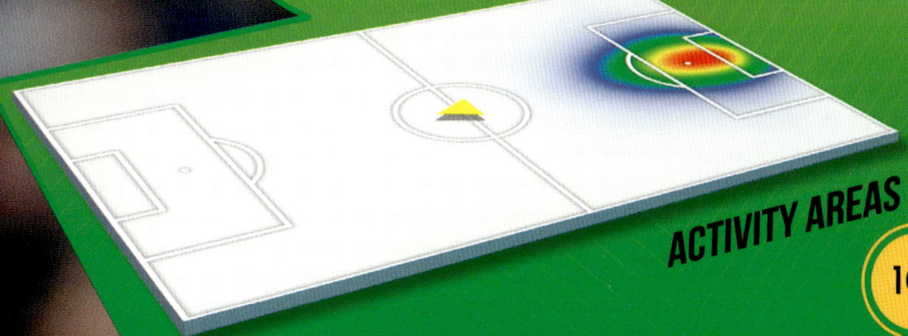

ACTIVITY AREAS

NATIONALITY
Switzerland

CURRENT CLUB
Inter Milan

YANN SOMMER

Reading the game is Sommer's special skill. The experienced Swiss goalkeeper stays calm under pressure, moves quickly across goal, and comes off his line to narrow the angle. He is not the tallest keeper, but his sharp positioning and quick clearances help launch attacks.

DATE OF BIRTH	DEC 17, 1988
POSITION	GOALKEEPER
HEIGHT	6 FT
PRO DEBUT	2005
PREFERRED FOOT	LEFT

MAJOR CLUB HONORS

⚽ Serie A: 2024, 2026 ⚽ UEFA Champions League: runner-up 2025 ⚽ Bundesliga: 2023 (Bayern Munich) ⚽ Coppa Italia: 2026

INTERNATIONAL HONORS

⚽ None to date

ACTIVITY AREAS

WOJCIECH SZCZĘSNY

After coming out of retirement to join Barcelona, Szczęsny showed he was still a sharp and reliable goalkeeper. He controls his penalty area, deals well with crosses, and reacts quickly to shots. With fast clearances and accurate passes, he can also launch counterattacks.

NATIONALITY
Poland

CURRENT CLUB
Barcelona

DATE OF BIRTH	APR 18, 1990
POSITION	GOALKEEPER
HEIGHT	6 FT, 5 IN
PRO DEBUT	2009
PREFERRED FOOT	RIGHT

GOALS CONCEDED 547

APPEARANCES 515

PENALTIES SAVED 17

SAVES 1,340

CLEAN SHEETS 183

PENALTIES FACED 84

PUNCHES 200

CATCHES 208

MAJOR CLUB HONORS

⚽ La Liga: 2025, 2026 ⚽ Serie A: 2018, 2019, 2020 (all Juventus) ⚽ Copa del Rey: 2025 ⚽ FA Cup: 2014, 2015 (all Arsenal) ⚽ Coppa Italia: 2018, 2021, 2024 (all Juventus)

INTERNATIONAL HONORS

⚽ None to date

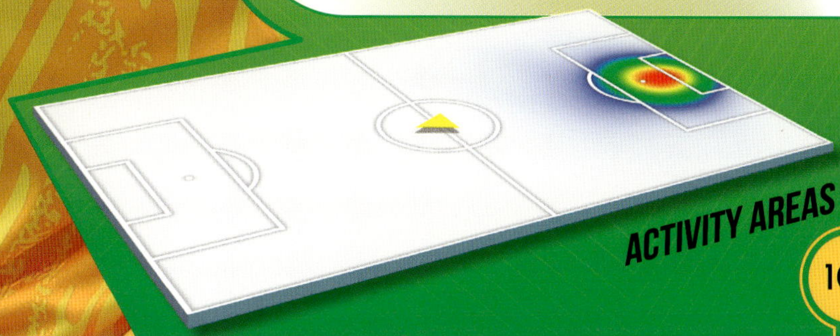

ACTIVITY AREAS

MANAGERS

Head coaches can shape a team as much as any star player. Some are tactical masterminds, choosing formations, pressing plans, and finding smart ways to attack. Others are brilliant leaders, building belief and getting the best from every player. They study opponents, make substitutions, and decide how their team should play in big moments. The coaches in this section have different styles, but most have one thing in common: they know how to win. Some lifted trophies as players before moving into management, while others made their name from the dugout.

WHAT DO THE STATS MEAN?

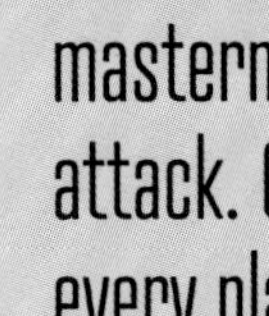

GAMES MANAGED

This is the number of games the coach has been in charge of across their entire career in soccer management.

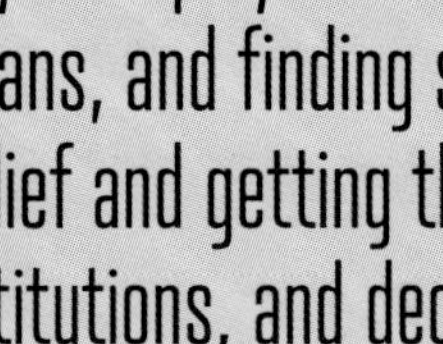

TEAMS MANAGED

The number of clubs (first teams only) that the coach has managed during their career to date.

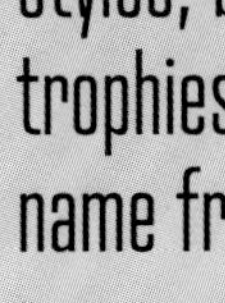

WINS

This is the number of games the coach has won, including one leg of a cup-tie, even if the tie was lost on aggregate or penalties.

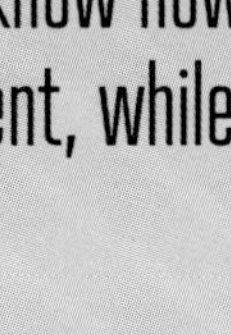

TROPHIES

The trophy list features the head coach's success in domestic top divisions, national and league cups, and international club competitions, except any super cups.

Did you know?

In the Champions League Era, Paris Saint-Germain's Luis Enrique is the second manager, after Zinedine Zidane, to win back-to-back European titles. He is also only the second manager to win the treble with two different clubs.

XABI ALONSO

NATIONALITY
Spain

CURRENT CLUB
Chelsea

After leading Bayer Leverkusen to their first Bundesliga title, Alonso became one of Europe's most exciting coaches. His teams are flexible, often building from the back before springing forward at speed. They press hard, counterattack quickly, and use wing-backs to create danger.

YEARS AS HEAD COACH: 6

FIRST CLUB: REAL SOCIEDAD B

CLUBS MANAGED	GAMES	LEAGUE TITLES
3	265	1
WINS	**DRAW**	**LOSSES**
147	59	59
CHAMPIONS LEAGUE TROPHIES	**EUROPA LEAGUE TROPHIES**	**OTHER TROPHIES**
0	0	2

MAJOR CLUB HONORS
- Bundesliga: 2024 (Bayer Leverkusen)
- DFB-Pokal: 2024 (Bayer Leverkusen)
- UEFA Europa League: runner-up 2024 (Bayer Leverkusen)

CARLO ANCELOTTI

NATIONALITY
Italy

CURRENT TEAM
Brazil

One of soccer's most decorated coaches, Ancelotti took charge of Brazil for the 2026 World Cup. Calm and flexible, he changes tactics to suit his players, rather than forcing one system. His teams stay organized, trust their stars, and strike quickly when chances appear.

YEARS AS HEAD COACH : 30

FIRST CLUB: REGGIANA

CLUBS MANAGED	GAMES	LEAGUE TITLES
10	1,401	6
WINS	**DRAW**	**LOSSES**
838	305	258
CHAMPIONS LEAGUE TROPHIES	**EUROPA LEAGUE TROPHIES**	**OTHER TROPHIES**
5	0	20

MAJOR CLUB HONORS
- La Liga: 2022, runner-up 2023, 2024 (all Real Madrid)
- UEFA Champions League: 2003, 2007 (all AC Milan), 2014, 2022, 2024 (all Real Madrid
- FIFA Club World Cup: 2007 (AC Milan), 2014, 2022 (all Real Madrid
- Serie A: 2004 (AC Milan)
- Premier League: 2010 (Chelsea)
- Ligue 1: 2013 (Paris St.-Germain)
- Copa del Rey: 2014, 2023 (all R. Mad.)
- Coppa Italia: 2003 (AC Milan)
- Bundesliga: 2017 (Bayern Munich)

MIKEL ARTETA

NATIONALITY
Spain

CURRENT CLUB
Arsenal

After years of careful rebuilding, Arteta led Arsenal to the 2025–26 Premier League title. His teams are intense, organized, and brave on the ball. They press high, defend strongly, and attack with smart movement, giving opponents danger to handle from all over the field.

YEARS AS HEAD COACH: 6

FIRST CLUB: ARSENAL

CLUBS MANAGED	GAMES	LEAGUE TITLES
1	353	1
WINS	**DRAW**	**LOSSES**
213	67	73
CHAMPIONS LEAGUE TROPHIES	**EUROPA LEAGUE TROPHIES**	**OTHER TROPHIES**
0	0	3

MAJOR CLUB HONORS

- Premier League: runner-up 2023, runner-up 2024, runner-up 2025, 2026
- UEFA Champions League: runner-up 2026
- FA Cup: 2020
- FA Community Shield: 2020, 2023

UNAI EMERY

NATIONALITY
Spain

CURRENT CLUB
Aston Villa

A Europa League expert, Emery led Aston Villa to their first major trophy in 30 years in 2026. His teams are detailed, disciplined, and hard to break down. They defend with shape, spring smart traps, and attack quickly when space opens up.

YEARS AS HEAD COACH: 21

FIRST CLUB: LORCA DEPORTIVA

CLUBS MANAGED	GAMES	LEAGUE TITLES
9	1,122	1
WINS	**DRAW**	**LOSSES**
602	240	280
CHAMPIONS LEAGUE TROPHIES	**EUROPA LEAGUE TROPHIES**	**OTHER TROPHIES***
0	5	6

*Excludes Super Cups

MAJOR CLUB HONORS

- UEFA Europa League: 2014, 2015, 2016 (all Sevilla), 2021 (Villareal), runner-up 2019 (Arsenal), 2026
- Ligue 1: 2018 (Paris Saint-Germain)
- Coupe de France: 2017, 2018 (all Paris Saint-Germain)

LUIS ENRIQUE

NATIONALITY
Spain

CURRENT CLUB
Paris Saint-Germain

After leading PSG to back-to-back Champions League titles, Luis Enrique proved his bold ideas could conquer Europe. His teams are brave on the ball, press together, and attack with freedom. He changes shape when needed, but always demands courage, teamwork, and control.

YEARS AS HEAD COACH: 14

FIRST CLUB: BARCELONA B

CLUBS MANAGED	GAMES	LEAGUE TITLES
5	554	5
WINS	**DRAW**	**LOSSES**
341	110	103
CHAMPIONS LEAGUE TROPHIES	**EUROPA LEAGUE TROPHIES**	**OTHER TROPHIES**
3	0	13

MAJOR CLUB HONORS
- UEFA Champions League; 2015 (Barcelona), 2025, 2026
- Ligue 1: 2024, 2025, 2026
- La Liga; 2015, 2016 (all Barcelona)
- FIFA World Club Cup; 2015 (Barcelona), runner-up 2025
- Coupe de France: 2024, 2025
- Copa del Rey; 2015, 2016, 2017 (all Barcelona)

HANSI FLICK

NATIONALITY
Germany

CURRENT CLUB
Barcelona

After his trophy-laden spell at Bayern Munich, Flick brought high-energy soccer to Barcelona. His teams press hard, defend with a high line, and attack quickly when they win the ball. In 2025–26, he guided Barça to a second straight La Liga title.

YEARS AS HEAD COACH: 29

FIRST CLUB: VICTORIA BAMMENTAL

CLUBS MANAGED	GAMES	LEAGUE TITLES
4	521	4
WINS	**DRAW**	**LOSSES**
290	98	133
CHAMPIONS LEAGUE TROPHIES	**EUROPA LEAGUE TROPHIES**	**OTHER TROPHIES**
1	0	7

MAJOR CLUB HONORS
- La Liga: 2025, 2026
- Supercopa de España: 2025, 2026
- Bundesliga: 2020, 2021 all (Bayern Munich)
- UEFA Champions League: 2020 (Bayern Munich)
- Copa del Rey: 2025
- DFB-Pokal: 2020 (Bayern Munich)
- FIFA Club World Cup: 2020 (Bayern Munich)
- UEFA Super Cup: 2020 (Bayern Munich)

GIAN PIERO GASPERINI

NATIONALITY
Italy

CURRENT CLUB
Roma

After transforming Atalanta into European winners, Gasperini took charge of Roma and led them back into the Champions League. His teams attack bravely but defend man-to-man, pressing opponents all over the field. Wing-backs push high to create overloads and make his 3–4–3 system dangerous.

YEARS AS HEAD COACH:	22
FIRST CLUB:	CROTONE

CLUBS MANAGED	GAMES	LEAGUE TITLES
6	935	0
WINS	**DRAW**	**LOSSES**
437	217	281
CHAMPIONS LEAGUE TROPHIES	**EUROPA LEAGUE TROPHIES**	**OTHER TROPHIES**
0	1	0

MAJOR CLUB HONORS
- UEFA Europa League: 2024

PEP GUARDIOLA

NATIONALITY
Spain

CURRENT CLUB
Free agent

A master of possession soccer, Guardiola changed the game with Barcelona, Bayern Munich, and Manchester City. His teams pass patiently, press fiercely, and attack with smart movement. After a trophy-filled decade at City, he prepared for one final season before stepping away.

YEARS AS HEAD COACH:	17
FIRST CLUB:	BARCELONA B

CLUBS MANAGED	GAMES	LEAGUE TITLES
4	1039	12
WINS	**DRAW**	**LOSSES**
741	164	134
CHAMPIONS LEAGUE TROPHIES	**EUROPA LEAGUE TROPHIES**	**OTHER TROPHIES**
3	0	26

MAJOR CLUB HONORS
- Premier League: 2018, 2019, 2021, 2022, 2023, 2024
- UEFA Champions League: 2009, 2011 Barcelona), runner-up 2021, 2023
- FIFA Club World Cup: 2009, 2011 (Barcelona), 2013 (B. Munich)
- La Liga: 2009, 2010, 2011 (Barcelona)
- Bundesliga: 2014, 2015, 2016 (B. Munich)
- FA Cup: 2019, 2023, 2026

EDDIE HOWE

After ending Newcastle's long wait for a major trophy, Howe became one of England's most respected coaches. His teams play with energy, pressing high to force mistakes and win the ball back quickly. In attack, they move fast, using width and runners from midfield.

NATIONALITY
England

CURRENT CLUB
Newcastle United

YEARS AS HEAD COACH: 17

FIRST CLUB: AFC BOURNEMOUTH

CLUBS MANAGED	GAMES	LEAGUE TITLES
3	776	0
WINS	**DRAW**	**LOSSES**
340	162	274
CHAMPIONS LEAGUE TROPHIES	**EUROPA LEAGUE TROPHIES**	**OTHER TROPHIES**
0	0	1

MAJOR CLUB HONORS

- EFL Cup: runner-up 2023, 2025

FABIAN HÜRZELER

After guiding Brighton to another top-half Premier League finish, Hürzeler signed a new deal until 2029. His teams play with high energy, pressing defenders near their own goal and passing forward quickly. They use the full width of the field to stretch opponents.

NATIONALITY
Germany

CURRENT CLUB
Brighton & Hove Albion

YEARS AS HEAD COACH: 11

FIRST CLUB: FC PIPINSRIED

CLUBS MANAGED	GAMES	LEAGUE TITLES
3	143	0
WINS	**DRAW**	**LOSSES**
74	37	32
CHAMPIONS LEAGUE TROPHIES	**EUROPA LEAGUE TROPHIES**	**OTHER TROPHIES**
0	0	1*

*Lower league

MAJOR CLUB HONORS

- 2. Bundesliga: 2024 (St. Pauli)

ANDONI IRAOLA

Iraola turns games into chaos for opponents. After making Bournemouth one of the Premier League's most exciting teams, he took the helm at Liverpool in 2026. His teams press aggressively, play forward quickly, and hunt for second balls, forcing defenders into rushed mistakes near their own goal.

NATIONALITY
Spain

CURRENT CLUB
Liverpool

YEARS AS HEAD COACH: 9

FIRST CLUB: AEK LARNACA

CLUBS MANAGED	GAMES	LEAGUE TITLES
4	312	0
WINS	**DRAW**	**LOSSES**
119	89	104
CHAMPIONS LEAGUE TROPHIES	**EUROPA LEAGUE TROPHIES**	**OTHER TROPHIES**
0	0	1*

*Lower league

MAJOR CLUB HONORS
- Cypriot Super Cup: 2018 (AELarnaca)

DIEGO SIMEONE

A fierce and long-serving coach at Atlético Madrid, Simeone builds teams that are tough, organized, and full of fight. They defend as a unit, battle for every ball, and are dangerous from set pieces. When space appears, they break forward quickly and attack with real purpose.

NATIONALITY
Argentina

CURRENT CLUB
Atlético Madrid

YEARS AS HEAD COACH: 18

FIRST CLUB: RACING CLUB

CLUBS MANAGED	GAMES	LEAGUE TITLES
6	1004	4
WINS	**DRAW**	**LOSSES**
564	225	215
CHAMPIONS LEAGUE TROPHIES	**EUROPA LEAGUE TROPHIES**	**OTHER TROPHIES**
0	2	4

MAJOR CLUB HONORS
- UEFA Champions League: runner-up 2014, 2016
- UEFA Europa League: 2012, 2018
- UEFA Super Cup: 2012, 2018
- La Liga: 2014, 2021
- Copa del Rey: 2013
- Primera División Apertura 2006 (Estudiantes)
- Primera División Clausura 2008 (Racing Club)

NOTES